Louis XIV

DAVID OGG

Louis XIV

OXFORD UNIVERSITY PRESS
London Oxford New York

Oxford University Press

OXFORD LONDON NEW YORK
GLASGOW TORONTO MELBOURNE WELLINGTON
CAPE TOWN IBADAN NAIROBI DAR ES SALAAM LUSAKA ADDIS ABABA
DELHI BOMBAY CALCUTTA MADRAS KARACHI LAHORE DACCA
KUALA LUMPUR SINGAPORE HONG KONG TOKYO

ISBN 0 19 888021 9

Selected Further Reading © OXFORD UNIVERSITY PRESS 1967

First published in the Home University Library *1933*
First issued as an Oxford University Press paperback 1967
This reprint 1973

PRINTED PHOTOLITHO IN GREAT BRITAIN BY J. W. ARROWSMITH LTD, BRISTOL

Contents

1
Early Years, 1638–61

THE OFFICIAL REIGN of Louis XIV (1654–1715) was only three years shorter than that of Queen Victoria. Both monarchs, closely associated with more than two generations of notable men and more than sixty years of great events, have given their names to distinctive epochs of modern history, and each reign had a confidence and spaciousness such as posterity may envy but can scarcely hope to emulate. There were certain common elements in the characters of the two sovereigns. Both were inspired by sincere and imperturbable piety; neither was of complicated intellectual structure; they had a high sense of duty to their office; and as they were regular and solicitous they succeeded in asserting themselves over subordinates. Each had clearly defined tastes, and subjects willing to be guided by these tastes; both took pride in the achievements of their peoples; and, as seen by a later age, they appear to embody many of the characteristic qualities of their race. Otherwise the two reigns present more material for contrast than for comparison.

Two great dynasties united in the creation of Louis XIV; for his mother Anne of Austria was the daughter of Philip III of Spain and so the granddaughter of the gloomy Philip of the Armada; while on his father's side he was the grandson of Henry of Navarre, the most beloved of all French monarchs. Louis was born at Saint-Germain on 26 August 1638, and became nominally king of France in 1643 on the death of his father Louis XIII. The attainment of his majority was pronounced on 28 August 1651 and, three years later, he was crowned at Rheims in the midst of a ritual the most majestic of all that solemnized the anointing of kings.

But his earliest associations were military rather than ecclesiastical, and among his first recollections must have been that of the pride and even emotion which greeted Condé's great victory at Rocroi (1643), when the Prince drove back an invading army from the frontier. This, one of the few decisive battles of the Thirty Years' War, thrilled contemporaries, since it marked the decline of Spain as a military power and the emergence of French prowess, incarnated in generals who at the time were distinguished more for dash and brilliance than for loyalty or endurance. Louis's early education helped to confirm this zeal for achievement. He was taught to admire Henry IV rather than Louis XIII; the heroism and godliness of Saint Louis were frequently cited by his preceptors, and he responded enthusiastically to the strictures which his teachers levelled at weak or puppet kings; but he was encouraged to seek for the evidence of Divine purpose not so much in the record of the past, as in the promise of his own future. The stimulus of good example was supplemented by the education usually given to princes at that time; namely, riding, dancing, and deportment; elementary mathematics (as an adjunct to the principles of fortification); biblical instruction, and a certain amount of classical knowledge, in which mythology preponderated. So conscientious were the efforts to make his upbringing an ideal one that text-books were compiled specially for his use; even the headings of his copy-books were adapted to his rank; for they included statements of the obedience due to sovereigns as the representatives of the Almighty. With the exception of *Don Quixote* there was no light reading in this curriculum.

Carefully planned as it was, Louis's education ignored many of the things that might have proved of interest to an intelligent ruler. The pupil learned little of geography; he knew less of recent history, and nothing at all of the financial or economic conditions of the country over which he was one day to rule. Nor were these omissions ever compensated for by travel. In this respect he was no exception among seventeenth-century monarchs; but the deficiency was to prove of special consequence, because his policy brought him into close contact with practically every state in Europe, and he was his own first minister. A contrast was provided by his cousin Charles of England who, while he had no book-learning, had derived much knowledge of men and countries from enforced foreign travel, and more than made up for lack of erudition by shrewdness and intelligence. Louis, not so fortunately endowed, was therefore obliged to base his policy on the information supplied by others.

The instructors of princes are generally enthusiastic about the abilities of their pupils. There was complete unanimity among those who had the privilege of shaping Louis's mind and character. From earliest years he was distinguished by a courtesy and graciousness of manner; he was of fair height, handsome, and active; he danced and acted to perfection; his conversation was marked by decision and good sense, and he showed that he was born to be a king. His piety was exemplary; he developed artistic taste and he was noteworthy for regularity and application. With the coming of adolescence his love-affairs produced some perturbation in the minds of those responsible for his welfare; but these need not have caused anxiety; for while they resulted from a certain exuberance or lavishness of temperament, they produced no disturbance in the securely-adjusted balance of his emotions. He was sensuous, but not inconveniently so; others may have suffered from his amours, but not he. More trouble came from the ample diet which he permitted himself. Like many Bourbons, he was a considerable eater, in spite of warning symptoms such as indigestion; but otherwise he had splendid health, and with years his royal person assumed greater amplitude and dignity. He had none of the humour or volatility of the French; his love for detail and routine savoured more of Madrid than of Paris; and the wax model made of him late in life by Benoïst shows distinctively Jewish features, derived perhaps from some Semitic element in his Spanish ancestry.

These receptive years were spent amid events which left a lasting impression on his mind. Of these, the most important was the Fronde. The word means a catapult; the Frondeurs were critics or opponents of the Government, and it was the outbreak in September 1648 of the First Fronde, or Fronde of the Parlement, which obliged Mazarin to conclude in haste the peace settlement of Westphalia (October 1648) which ended the Thirty Years' War. Briefly, the causes of the movement were these. The Parlement of Paris was not a parliament in the English sense, but was really a combined tribunal and legal incorporation to which political power had long since been denied; moreover, it represented not the nation, but the legal profession in Paris. Its magistrates and councillors were recruited from the wealthier *bourgeoisie*, a class which suffered much from the depredations of the Italian minister Mazarin, who had become a multi-millionaire by skilful juggling with the national finances; indeed, his jewels, his richly-bound books and manuscripts, his gold plate and chests of bullion were the profits derived principally from the process of rigging the market in national securities. The securities consisted mainly of *Rentes*, or government annuities; and, except that they were administered by the municipality of Paris, they were a national obligation; a stock intended not to be speculative, but to provide the moderate and steady yield of a gilt-edged security. Widows, orphans, and charitable corporations were dependent on the revenue from these funds, which were therefore of special importance not to the noble, nor the peasant, nor the gambler; but to the average burgess, anxious to secure a dependable return on his capital, or to make provision for his dependants.

Mazarin and those confederate with him manipulated the *Rentes*, as they were able to do because the Government controlled the payment of interest. By withholding this interest as long as possible, the price was forced down, when large blocks could be bought cheaply; interest was at last paid; the stock rose, and the holdings were then unloaded as a preliminary to repetition of the process. The great European war in which France was engaged served to distract national attention from this abuse. It would be harsh to say that Mazarin was a cheat; he was really a great cardinal-diplomatist, profiting by a most complicated and wasteful financial system; he believed that God was the author of all good things, and why should he reject them when they fell into his lap? By discretion and secrecy he avoided scandal; also, he studiously withheld all instruction in national finance from his pupil Louis. So the widows and orphans were despoiled, and their *bourgeois* relatives swore vengeance on this foreign ecclesiastic, whose courtesy was his only substitute for a conscience. The result of this and other misdeeds (mainly financial) was an attempt at revolution. Meeting in the Chamber of St. Louis the various sections of the Paris Parlement combined in July 1648 to formulate a charter of constitutional rights, including securities for the liberty of the subject and more regular control over finance and taxation. Mazarin and the Court appeared to yield; then when news came of another victory by

Condé, an order was given for the arrest of the leaders (August 1648). If the Parlement hoped to emulate the English Parliament, Mazarin and Anne of Austria would try the methods of the Stuarts.

A rising in Paris in which there was much street fighting but little concerted action caused the Court to give way a second time; the imprisoned magistrates were released (October 1648) and reforms were again promised. Meanwhile the treaties of Westphalia were signed, and French soldiers and generals were available for the crushing of dissent at home. In January 1649 Anne summoned the Parlement to meet at Montargis, where it would be directly under the control of the Court. The enforced flitting thus imposed on the home-loving magistrates of Paris was indeed a harsh punishment, and the summons was treated as a declaration of war; accordingly, the city was put into a state of defence and for nearly three months (January–March 1649) was besieged by Condé and royalist troops. It was a mock-heroic siege, and ended in a compromise, the treaty of Rueil, by which concessions were again made on behalf of a Court determined to gain time by yielding.

Unfortunately the movement did not end here; for the infection of rebellion soon spread to the princes and the nobility, with the result that during the next three years France was plunged in the anarchy known as the Second Fronde, or Fronde of the Princes. The Princes were the great Condé, first prince of the blood (1621–86), the victor of Rocroi, troublesome, brilliant, and arrogant; his younger brother Conti, and his brother-in-law the Duke of Longueville; there was Gaston, Duke of Orléans, a younger brother of Louis XIII, who felt obliged to take a part; there were also notable women, such as the Duchess of Longueville, and Mademoiselle de Montpensier, a cousin of Louis XIV, anxious to marry him. A stage-manager was found in the coadjutor of the Archbishop of Paris, John Francis Paul de Gondi, who wanted to be a cardinal and so first minister. The Second Fronde, really the recoil of the French nobility from the repression to which they had been subjected by Richelieu, was led by men who wished to exercise a power inconsistent with the prerogative of monarchy; its campaigns and sieges provided opportunity for display and showmanship, mostly at the expense of the peasants whose fields were harried, or of the burgesses whose shops were looted; and its climax came in February 1651 when, for a brief moment, the two Frondes united. At a convention held in the Luxembourg by their representatives, the summoning of the States-General was demanded; the Queen Regent was to be sent to a nunnery, and the young King was to rule with the advice of a council chosen from the three Estates. At this point, had the nobility and the *bourgeoisie* been capable of joint action they might have enforced these demands, which would have entirely altered the constitution; but the two castes had only to be brought into contact in order to realize how deep were their antipathies to each other, and Mazarin in exile knew that he would be saved by the dissensions among his enemies. Thereafter, the movement slowly worked itself out in spectacular forays and ineffective campaigns, in which the Court was as often the quarry as the hunter; but by the end of 1652 hostilities had ceased, and in February of the following year Mazarin was welcomed back to France by a nation tired of anarchy.

During these troubles there were moments when Louis and his mother were little better than prisoners, and their future seemed at the mercy of a mob. The mob might be the Paris hooligans or the French nobility; the distinction was not then a profound one. Inevitably, Louis retained a vivid impression of these events, and his policy as a ruler was to some extent determined by them. Most marked was his dislike of Paris; so he afterwards deserted the Louvre and set up the headquarters of the French monarchy at Versailles. Secondly, he realized the danger from over-mighty subjects; hence his policy of reducing them from potentates to courtiers and even flunkeys; for which purpose Versailles proved a most effective institution. Thirdly, he acquired a rooted antipathy to *rentiers*. Their grievances were probably never explained to him; but he could not dissociate them from the Fronde; nor did he perceive how, with a little encouragement and good faith, he might have procured money from them on cheaper terms than from any other class.

Other consequences may be attributed to the Frondes. Whatever their causes and results, these episodes seemed like echoes of the great Civil War struggle in England. In Italy, Spanish rule had (in 1647) been contested by the revolt of Masaniello in Naples; Germany was exhausted from the Thirty Years' War; Russia, emerging from the Time of Troubles was not yet consolidated under the Romanoffs; Sweden had a girl queen who, in 1654, resigned her crown; Poland, under its elective kingship, was only nominally a monarchy, and was really a permanent illustration of anarchy; Spain was still a monarchy, but its King, Philip IV, and his successor, Charles II, were the victims of racial decline. Throughout Europe, personal monarchy was either undeveloped, or discredited, or abolished, and men were experimenting in other types of government. Now, an institution is all the stronger if, during a period of its abeyance, its necessity can be demonstrated. This was true of absolute sovereignty. It derived its theoretical sanction from Divine decree, and its practical justification from the unsettlement and disunion which then followed constitutional experiment. Not progress, but uniformity was the lesson to be deduced from the experience of change and variation; internal peace was the most obvious advantage to be gained from the rule of the strong, legitimate king. This is the explanation of the absolutism of Louis XIV; unfortunately the internal peace which it secured for France was not accorded to Europe.

From such set-backs France needed a long period of recuperation. By his suavity and assiduity Mazarin did much to procure this; and the continued successes of French arms helped to restore national prestige. Early in 1657 he allied with Cromwell and the two powers then concentrated their forces against Dunkirk, Mardyk, and Gravelines in the Spanish Netherlands. After the Battle of the Dunes (June 1658) Louis made a triumphal entry into Dunkirk, and in terms of the agreement the port was handed over to England. By such successes Mazarin forced Spain to come to terms, which were embodied in the Treaty of the Pyrenees (November 1659) whereby one more stage in the struggle was ended. By this treaty France acquired Roussillon, at the south-eastern extremity of the Pyrenees, and the greater part of Artois on the north-eastern frontier, together with Landrecies and Gravelines in Flanders; and (in Lorraine) two towns hitherto under the suzerainty of the Spanish possession of Luxembourg, namely, Thionville and Montmédy. Most important of all was the marriage contract whereby Maria Theresa, elder of the two daughters of Philip IV, was betrothed to Louis, on the express stipulation that she should resign all claim to the Spanish Succession in consideration of the payment of a dowry of 500,000 crowns. There was no clear understanding of what were Maria Theresa's claims to the Spanish Succession, as Philip might yet have a son (his son Charles was born in 1661); nor did the use of the phrase in the treaty imply any recognition by Spain of the legitimacy of a claim by Maria Theresa to the whole or part of the Succession. The clause was framed by one of Mazarin's subordinates, and was cleverly framed, because it implied a contract whereby there was a surrender of rights in return for a dowry. As the dowry was never paid, these fictive rights became concrete things to be vindicated by war.

Tribute is commonly paid to this cleverness of French diplomacy which, by coupling a surrender of 'rights' with the promise of a money payment that probably could not be fulfilled, succeeded in creating rights out of negative quantities. Nevertheless, there was an element of superfluity about it all. The treaty, by strengthening the French frontier, continued the best traditions of Richelieu; but did not bring to the Bourbons any legitimate footing in the Spanish Succession; indeed, it was absurd to expect that a treaty should confer such an advantage at a time when the King of Spain was not yet forty years of age and might well have an heir. Mazarin knew that Spain was too poor to find the money for the dowry; but he could not have been so foolish as to suppose that the 'claims' thereby acquired would be recognized by any free tribunal in Europe; obviously they would have to be enforced by arms, and the quibble would become a syllogism only when spaced out by artillery. The marriage, so far from being a bond of union between the two countries, was really a further cause of quarrel; and so the shy Spanish girl who crossed the Pyrenees in June 1660 brought with her, not a dowry, but provocative marriage lines. Bride and bridegroom did not have to submit for long to the paternal guidance of Mazarin; for that great man died early in 1661, in an atmosphere of piety and abundance, leaving two nieces who devoted themselves to the task of spending his fortune.

2

Europe in 1661

It is the true greatness of Louis XIV that, by his activities, the history of his reign was, in a real sense the history of Europe, and that Versailles became in policy what Rome had been in religion. For this reason it is necessary to preface the account of these activities by a brief survey of the chief European states at the time of his accession.

The Papacy provided a good illustration of adaptation to environment. Now that rival faiths were firmly established in Christendom, and since many Catholics hesitated to accept the supremacy of the Pope in all matters, spiritual and temporal, it was necessary for the leader of Catholicism to walk warily and avoid giving offence. As the supreme Pontiffs could not yet shelter behind their infallibility, they had to resort to diplomacy, a profession in which the Church provided the best training, Mazarin being one of the most famous pupils of this school. It was the diplomacy of a household slowly piecing together what was left after the depredations of hostile neighbours; there were, it is true, plenty of offensive weapons in the house, but it was feared that they had lost their efficacy; some prestige remained, however, and this might have been of service wherever the Holy See was called in as umpire. That the Papacy was no longer a political force is axiomatic; but it is not so certain that this was an unmixed blessing for Europe; because, after all, the Vatican represented an alternative to brute force, and in the past there had been times when peace was preserved either by fear of its anathema or by appeal to its verdict. But this prerogative was gone; and to complete its impotence, there was needed only public humiliation; this it suffered at the hands of Louis XIV. In 1661 the Pope was Fabio Chigi, Alexander VII; an old and cautious man, not too resentful of insult.

The Holy Roman Empire had receded from Germany, as already from Italy; in effect, therefore, the powers of the Habsburg emperors were coterminous with their temporal possessions, which were mainly in Austria, Bohemia, and western Hungary. Since the fifteenth century the emperors had invariably been selected from the House of Habsburg by the College of Electors, who, in 1661, consisted of the Archbishops of Mainz, Cologne, and Trier; the Duke of Bavaria; the Margraves of Saxony and Brandenburg, the Elector Palatine of the Rhine, and the King of Bohemia (this last title was in Habsburg possession). The Emperor ruled with the help of a deliberative body or Diet representing the Electors, Princes, and Imperial Towns, which generally met at Ratisbon, where much time was spent in formal procedure, and few matters of international importance were discussed. Though still under the nominal suzerainty of Vienna, the German states (in number more than 300) were now almost completely autonomous, and were limited only by the obligation not to enter into alliances against the Emperor. In effect, therefore, the Empire, like the Papacy, had lost its old pre-eminence; but on the other hand, the Austrian Habsburgs were a great political power and this for three reasons; namely, the connexion with their Spanish cousins; their extensive dominions in central and eastern Europe, and because these possessions presented a bulwark against the encroachments of the Turk. Though unscrupulous with minorities and dominated by a priestly obscurantism, the Habsburgs at this time were not aggressive, having enough to occupy themselves in ruling their hordes of Germans, Czechs, and Magyars, and holding their own against the Ottoman. Their dynasty was represented in 1661 by Leopold I, who, as his rule began in 1658 and ended in 1705, was almost exactly contemporary with his cousin Louis XIV. He was a man of mild and somewhat timorous character, fervidly religious; easily dominated by stronger personalities, and always apprehensive of anything threatening to disturb the delicately-poised balance on which his dominion rested.

A more settled rule was that in Spain, the Catholic monarchy, ruled in 1661 by Philip IV, the last-but-one of the Spanish Habsburgs. His kingdom was the nucleus of a great empire, eagerly watched by younger nations anxious for its dissolution. Among its possessions in Europe were the southern Netherlands, roughly equivalent to the modern Belgium; a great part of Italy, including the Milanese, Naples, and Sicily; the islands of Majorca, Minorca, and Sardinia. In North Africa, Oran, Melilla, and Ceuta were Spanish; as were the Canary Islands and the Philippines; also Central America, with Panama and Mexico; the whole of South America, except Guiana and Brazil; islands in the West Indies, including Cuba and San Domingo. The geographical distribution of her European possessions was of special importance. By her Italian territories Spain dominated northern Italy and was powerful in the Mediterranean; she controlled the Straits of Gibraltar, and had an old claim to Tangier, which was in English possession between 1661 and 1684; in the southern Netherlands she had a wedge dividing France from the Dutch; while on France's eastern frontier she had both Luxembourg and Franche Comté. The result was that, either directly, or with the help of small allied or neutral states such as Lorraine and Savoy, Spain could threaten France on her least defensible frontier—that is, on the east and north-east. But the military and economic decline of Spain had considerably reduced the menace from this source; for by 1661 the Spanish Empire could with difficulty be held together by its impoverished Government. So far from launching on new conquests or threatening the security of neighbours, the statesmanship of the peninsula was engaged in keeping these scattered possessions together, suppressing heretics at home and excluding foreigners from the colonial trade. Another cause of weakness was the long struggle with Portugal. The Portuguese were fighting for their independence, which they achieved by 1665; hence it was the policy of the enemies of Spain to ally with Portugal.

Among the more enterprising nations were the English and the Dutch. Charles II was restored to the English throne in 1660, as the result of a spontaneous and effusive reaction against Puritan rule. No conditions of any kind were imposed on him; he was given control of the armed forces of the country, and he was free to direct his foreign policy. But Charles could not raise taxes without consent of Parliament; and the hereditary revenue granted to him for his lifetime was at first inadequate for even the normal peace-time administration. As this dependence on Parliament proved irksome, he was the more willing to be subsidized by Louis; not that he was over wholly dependent on the French King; but the subsidy made the difference between comfort and economy. Charles's one motive in life was comfort. In 1661 it might well have seemed that England was fitted only to be a tributary to France, because of these characteristics: there was no army worthy of the name; Englishmen hated the sight of a red-coat; the King was neither pious, nor ambitious, nor even industrious, and was dependent for supplementary supplies on an assembly of critics known as the Parliament; moreover, the kingdom was divided by heretics and republicans, and the Government was occupied mainly in the work of enforcing ostracism on the dissenters. From the continental point of view, therefore, England was not a 'well-conditioned' state. Properly led, however, it seemed that English manpower might be of service abroad; the English Navy had always to be reckoned with; but otherwise England was to be patronized rather than feared. Such was the attitude which Louis was encouraged to adopt towards England; he was not disillusioned by Charles, who needed the money.

Another example of a trading and heretic race was the Dutch. The Seven Provinces had secured Spanish recognition of their independence in 1648; but long before then the Dutch, by their enterprise and tolerance had laid the foundations of the most prosperous overseas trade achieved in the century, and in doing so they acted on two contrary maxims. On the British and Greenland coasts it was freedom of the seas—that is, a right to take part in the herring and whale industries, in spite of prior rights claimed by others; but in the East Indies and on the Gold Coast it was the opposite principle, for there they claimed prescriptive rights, and forced out every competitor. As they had no superfluous population and did not penalize religious disentients they had no need for overseas settlements as dumping grounds; except in Java and in the New Netherlands, they had trading stations rather than colonies, and their commerce was assisted by a network of agents and middlemen all over the globe; moreover, with their great mercantile marine they could provide quick and efficient transport for the goods of others. Their success was due to the fact that against seventeenth-century competitors they were using twentieth-century methods; for they were more interested in national prosperity than in religion; they built their ships on mass-production methods; they knew how to pack the goods they handled; and with Teutonic pertinacity they always sought out and monopolized the best markets. Their example caused at first irritation, then emulation; defeated rivals called them upstarts and ended by copying their methods. The English proved admirable pupils; but Louis XIV could never quite bring himself to enrol himself among their disciples, and his dislike of their character was to prove of some consequence in his foreign policy. This is why he preferred to be cheated by Charles II than by the Dutch.

France had helped the United Provinces in their struggle for independence, and Louis naturally expected that they would show some measure of gratitude. But their constitution was unacceptable to him; for it was a federation of burgher oligarchies masquerading under the name of a republic. Nevertheless, the House of Orange was still in being, and much might therefore be hoped from the young Prince William, if the rule of the great Pensionary John de Witt could be set aside. In this matter there was a distinct cleavage in Dutch opinion; the seamen of Zealand being whole-heartedly for the cause of Orange, while the rich merchants of Holland and Amsterdam preferred their independence. So Louis showed a paternal solicitude for the young Prince, in the hope that by the restoration of his line, and its elevation to monarchist (that is, absolutist) status, the Dutch might be forced out of their 'republicanism' and introduced into the society of respectable states. Hence, like England, the Dutch Provinces did not quite fit into the scheme of things as visualized in 1661 by Louis; but their case was not hopeless; for they might be educated; and, if they proved obstinate, they could be annihilated.

In the Baltic, France had a more willing ally in Sweden, a country which played a decisive part in seventeenth-century history. The Vasa kings had given an epic character to the destinies of their nation; and their heroic exploits are still the theme of enthusiastic commemoration. Christina's reign (1648–54) was an interlude; her successor, Charles X, continued the traditional policy of warfare with Denmark, and anticipated the eighteenth-century partitions by invading Poland, which he proposed to divide with his partner, the Elector of Brandenburg. After his death, the north of Europe was pacified by the two treaties of Oliva and Copenhagen (May and June 1660), the general effect of which was that the King of Poland renounced his claim to the Swedish throne; the Elector of Brandenburg withdrew his troops from Sweden's territories in

Germany; Denmark recovered some of her lost possessions, and
Sweden added to hers the provinces of Scania, Bleking, and Halland.
Thereupon followed a period of recuperation in Sweden; and during
the minority and reign of Charles XI there was comparative
peace in the north; though her possession of Western Pomerania
dragged Sweden into German politics. Until 1682 Sweden remained
a faithful ally of France.

Other states whose alliance was valued by Louis were Brandenburg, Poland, and Turkey. The first of these, under the rule of the
Hohenzollern electors, was steadily developing from a duchy to a
kingdom. Of these electors the most notable was Frederick William
(1640–88), whose two main objects were to unite his scattered
possessions into an organized state, and to train an army for intervention in the quarrels of his neighbours. In both objects he succeeded. Industry and commerce were encouraged; foreign farmers
and artisans were introduced; a civil service was created, and the
whole was welded together under a military aristocracy, controlled
by the Elector. By the Treaty of Westphalia (1648) he had obtained
eastern Pomerania (mainly through the help of France); thereafter
he thrust his dominion east and west; on the one side into east Prussia,
on the other into the territories of Cleve and Jülich. Frederick
William was an eager recipient of French money; he had an army of
30,000 men; he was the most ambitious prince of Germany, the
most effective lever among the Teutonic states against the Emperor.
Louis XIV was the fairy godmother of Prussia.

Conditions in Poland did not seem so easily calculable as in
Brandenburg or Sweden; for there the social and economic conditions
were quite unlike those prevailing in western Europe, where events
had favoured the development of administrative machinery, and the
creation of concentrated and absolutist monarchies. In Poland
there were two anomalies which together were responsible for
chronic anarchy—an elective kingship and the sanctity of minorities. Polish history was therefore not unlike that of some South
American republics, except that there was more interference from
outside. Not unnaturally, Louis interested himself in Polish affairs,
and for each election there was generally a French candidate;
indeed, at the election of 1668 there were two, but the native noble
Michael Wisniowiecki was elected, and as King he maintained the
Austrian connexion, which was also dominant in the reign of his

successor, John Sobieski. French diplomacy was more successful in Turkey, where a commercial footing had been secured early in the preceding century, a connexion of great importance to France, since Turkish power in Europe was then more extensive than it is today; for the territory recognizing the suzerainty of the Sultan included what are now the Balkan states, with Moldavia, Transylvania, and a great part of Hungary. In 1664 the military reputation of the Turks suffered a reverse by their defeat at St. Gothard on the Raab. Thereafter the Ottoman Empire was generally considered to be in a state of decline, and so opponents sometimes underestimated its strength. This may account in part for the unexpectedness of the revival under Sultan Mohammed IV (1648–87) and the Kiuprili grand viziers; indeed, had it not been for their reverse before the walls of Vienna in 1683 the Turks might well have overrun the whole of central Europe. In the Mediterranean their power had also to be reckoned with; this became more formidable in 1669 when, after a siege which had lasted more than twenty years, Candia (Crete) was captured from Venice. To Louis, the Ottoman was a valuable ally because of the incessant Turkish campaigns against the eastern territories of Leopold, and because the alliance ensured the economic preponderance of France in Syria and the Levant.

Such, very briefly, were the most important of the states with which France was brought into contact by the policy of Louis XIV. It is now necessary to allude to the question of frontiers. A glance at the map will show how, in 1661, the neighbours of France included these territories: (a) those belonging to Spain, (b) those still bound by some degree of allegiance to the Emperor, and (c) those owned by certain small, independent states. In regard to the first category, there was the Franco-Spanish frontier constituted by the Pyrenees. This had already been strengthened by the acquisition of Navarre and Béarn, the patrimony of Henry IV, and by the addition of Roussillon, acquired by the Treaty of the Pyrenees; in consequence of these adjustments, the south-western frontier was approximated more closely to the mountain barrier. At the other extremity of France were the Spanish possessions of the Low Countries, with Luxembourg and Franche Comté. As regards the second category, that of lands still bound, however nominally, to the Emperor, the most notable were the Rhenish Palatinate and certain parts of

Alsace, including the Imperial city of Strasbourg. In the third category, that of the small, independent states, were Lorraine, the Swiss Confederation, and Savoy. The Swiss managed to preserve their neutrality; but this was more difficult for the dukes of Savoy and Lorraine, who at times were practically forced to choose between a French and a Spanish alliance.

It was the eastern and north-eastern frontier which was to prove of special consequence because it was not delimited by any continuous natural barrier, and there the Spanish territories were linked with those nominally subject to the Emperor, an association all the more formidable as Spain possessed the whole of the Milanese, and could move her troops into Germany through the Valtelline. On this side, therefore, France might be menaced by an alliance of the Spanish and Imperial Habsburgs. This was first recognized in 1552 when France acquired the three Lorraine bishoprics of Metz, Toul, and Verdun, and thereby transferred the strategic centre of the struggle from the Po and the Adige to the Meuse and Moselle. The policy of defending France on her continental border was continued by Richelieu and Mazarin. By the Treaty of Westphalia (1648) France acquired full sovereignty over the greater part of Alsace, thereby reaching the Rhine; the treaty of the Pyrenees added Arras and almost all of Artois, thereby assimilating what was formerly a small enclave; and by the same treaty the terminus of the frontier was extended to Gravelines (to Dunkirk, by the purchase of the port from England in 1662); while in Lorraine the outposts of Thionville and Montmédy (formerly pertaining to Luxembourg) became French. Thus, in the century preceding 1661 the frontier changes had been mainly rectifications; and though these involved the inclusion of some non-French speaking peoples, they had the justification that in some cases they brought the frontier to what was then a natural barrier, and in others they eliminated projections of alien territory. But it was clear that at several points, especially in Lorraine and Flanders, a satisfactory settlement had not yet been reached.

This indeterminate condition of affairs was to be found elsewhere. On the south-east the frontier stopped short of Nice, then part of the dukedom of Savoy. East of the lower reaches of the Rhône were two small territories—Avignon and Orange—the first a papal possession, the second claimed by several noble houses. Orange became French in 1713, Avignon in 1791; meanwhile the geographical position of the latter possession gave to the French kings a convenient weapon for use against the Papacy; namely, the threat of annexation. If now the eastern frontier be followed from the south, it will be seen that the Maritime, French, and Swiss Alps provided geographical obstacles, and that control of mountain passes was an essential of strategy. French armies had on several occasions entered Piedmont by the Mont Cenis Pass, and Richelieu had already purchased from Savoy the outlying fortress of Pignerol (Pinerolo), about twenty miles south-west of Turin; farther east, the stronghold of Casale was annexed by Louis in 1681. On this side, therefore, France could threaten Spanish domination in northern Italy; but on the other hand she might be attacked by Savoy. To the north, the Jura presents some opportunities for a natural delimitation; here a frontier was established by Louis's acquisition of Franche Comté in 1678. Still farther north, the Rhine valley supplied a natural limit on the eastern flank of Alsace; this was vastly strengthened by the acquisition of Strasbourg in 1681. West of Alsace was the independent duchy of Lorraine, separating France from the frontier which she had acquired on the Rhine; but here there were strong, though isolated centres of French influence; and though Louis never succeeded in adding Lorraine to his obedience, he made the position of its duke an impossible one, and steadily absorbed some of his territories. The same policy was pursued in Luxembourg; but unlike Lorraine, Luxembourg never became a French possession. In Lorraine, the policy of Louis can be justified on the ground that the duchy divided France from her frontier; also, whatever opinion may be entertained of the aggressions of Louis XIV, it is true that in the conquered provinces French rule was comparatively tactful and enlightened.

It was at the north-eastern corner of Alsace where the Rhine enters the Lower or Rhenish Palatinate that that frontier ceased to bear any conformity with natural or geographical features, because from that point it turns west and north-west, and is separated from the Rhine by an increasingly broad belt of territory, in which were then included a part of the Lower Palatinate, the lands of Jülich, the whole of the Spanish Netherlands, and a southern portion of the United Provinces. Assuming that in this corner of Europe the Rhine would have provided a natural barrier, it is clear that France was separated from it by lands in which it was difficult to find any intermediate or secondary frontier; for the wedge is divided by three river-valleys, those of the Moselle, the Meuse, and the Scheldt, which stretch predominantly north-east and south-west; and therefore, as they cut across the frontier, they provide not impediments, but avenues of penetration. In regard therefore to this all-important sector, the policy of an enterprising French king might well have been All, and of a cautious king Nothing; All, that is, the conquest of the wedge and the extension of the frontier to the Rhine; Nothing, in the sense that the existing frontier might have been retained and strengthened for defence. Either policy might have succeeded; the first, by the tremendous predominance of French military resources; the second, because in the reign of Louis XIV, neither Spain nor the Emperor was aggressive, and so there was ample opportunity for consolidating this artificial frontier by the erection of forts, and good reason to hope that, whether from negotiation or inheritance, its limits would be extended. Historians would hesitate to approve either alternative, and most of them would condemn the second as pusillanimous; though, in the light of later events, it would have proved the best expedient.

Louis's actual policy was neither All nor Nothing, but a compromise—marriages and sieges. He based his claim to scattered fractions of the Spanish Netherlands on his marriage with Maria Theresa, and conducted numerous sieges in those territories, so that France gained such important possessions as Lille, Valenciennes, and Cambrai; but the vital question of the frontier was left practically untouched. Similar was his policy in the Palatinate—the alliance, by a second marriage of his brother, with the family of the Elector, which gave him a shadowy claim to some possessions in the Electorate; but in addition to sieges there were devastations, both conducted with scientific thoroughness. The sieges gave Louis a great military reputation, and the devastations made his name feared and hated throughout Europe; but it is not so clear that either of these things brought the question of the frontier any nearer to a solution; and it is certain that most of the gains in Flanders and the Palatinate had to be surrendered at the Treaty of Ryswick (1697), by which time Louis had conclusively proved that neither by arms nor by diplomacy could he make any substantial progress in these border territories. Then (in 1700) by the will of Charles II, the whole of the Spanish Netherlands (with other territories) was conferred on Louis's grandson; in other words, the greater part of the wedge was placed under French influence, and so the problem was suddenly brought within sight of solution. Europe acquiesced, though not enthusiastically, in this unexpected settlement; whereupon Louis so irritated his neighbours by violent and incautious measures that he had to fight for the inheritance, and lost the greater part of it. It is not surprising, therefore, that responsible French historians are unable to find any trace of purpose or consistency in the policy adopted by Louis XIV for this all-important part of his frontier.

But this discussion has proceeded on the assumption that Louis felt the need for a more securely-defended frontier and strove to obtain it. Neither his *Memoirs* nor his correspondence provide any support for this assumption; on the contrary, Louis approached the problem not from the starting-point of national security, but of personal reputation and the extension of French influence; and the only contemporary who appears to have thought of the problem of defence was Vauban. It would be idle to condemn Louis on the ground of his inability to perceive that France might one day be obliged to exchange the offensive for the defensive; but on the other hand it is definitely untrue that his wars had for their object the attainment of national security. In the course of his wars he captured outlying fortresses such as Freiburg, Breisach, and Philippsburg; by purchase and annexation France had also acquired Pignerol and Casale; but the cost of upkeep entailed by these places was out of all proportion to their strategic value, and their retention helped to make the French frontier still more artificial. This was the opinion of Vauban, who was in the unique position that, while more than any other man he was the agent by which Louis scored his military successes, he yet expressed regret that these successes were not dictated by any coherent policy, and still left Paris and the north-eastern frontier dangerously exposed.

Such, very briefly, was the state of Europe and of the French frontiers in the earlier years of Louis XIV. Before narrating the course of Louis's diplomacy and wars it is necessary to allude to certain general considerations which had some influence on international relations. First of all diplomacy, though an old art, was a comparatively new profession and in this period was sometimes

confused with espionage. The maintenance of peace was not a
professed object of the diplomatic agent; rather he was concerned
to preserve the prestige of his master, and was always on the alert
for anything implying a diminution of that prestige. Secrecy and
surprise were also of importance; indeed, diplomatic activities
were often little more than a contest in deception; and an ambassador might use his immunities in order to foment treason and
disaffection in the state where he served. In this way diplomacy
helped to intensify that atmosphere of tension and distrust which,
more than anything else, is responsible for European war.

Louis had the services of a large and carefully-chosen personnel
for his diplomacy; no other state could boast so many representatives
and agents. Thus, for Italy there were three ambassadors, allotted
to Rome, Venice, and Turin; at other places in Italy, as also in
Germany, there were residents; and in each of these countries,
Denmark, Sweden, Poland, Holland, England, Spain, and Turkey,
there was an ambassador. A high standard was exacted from these
men; after 1679, when Louis determined to effect an even closer
supervision of policy, they had to send more detailed reports; and
the instructions issued for their observance are models of thoroughness and lucidity. Louis's representatives were invariably men who
could mix freely at the Courts to which they were accredited; they
were specially chosen for the service or country assigned to them;
they knew French and Latin, but rarely the native language of the
country to which they were sent. This handicap sometimes severely
restricted the sources from which they could draw their information;
moreover, experience showed that while these agents were always
quick to snatch an advantage, they did not have the shrewdness
and intuition so characteristic of the Venetian ambassadors. The
result was that, while the information on which Louis acted was
always voluminous and detailed, it represented a partial and in
some cases distorted aspect of the truth. His diplomacy knew
everything about the vices of Courts and nothing about the virtues
of Nations.

A second effect may be attributed to the linguistic difficulty;
namely, that it helped to increase the uncertainty of international
relations. Latin was still used by educated men, and was the
language of scientific and technical books; but it was steadily
yielding to the national languages of Europe, all of which were

already accumulating literatures of their own. In proportion as the use of international Latin declined, and as younger languages were adapted to the new needs, so it became more difficult to convey in words a shade of meaning which would have exactly the same significance for two men of different speech. Even if Latin were used, the same difficulty was experienced; because the new vocabularies had so outstripped the old universal one that the latter was becoming inadequate for the expression of characteristically modern conceptions, and its use was therefore responsible for much misunderstanding and dispute. For this reason an inconvenient treaty did not always have to be repudiated, since it was generally easy so to interpret its terms as to provide some pretext for evasion; and the result was a tendency to read into the terms of 'perpetual alliances' meanings which might be inconsistent with the intentions of the original signatories. The diplomacy of Louis XIV illustrated how easily such pretexts for evasion could be found.

Diplomacy was influenced also by the fact that in the Europe of Louis's earlier days the personal sovereign was sole master of his foreign policy. International relations therefore provided monarchs with an opportunity for self-expression; and, as those early kings who had created states were known to have been men of valour, so their successors were assumed to be men of more than ordinary ability. Moreover, many kings still thought of power in terms of territory, rather than of money or trading advantage; and therefore the acquisition of a province was a good thing, not merely because national frontiers might be extended thereby, but because these enlargements enhanced the personal reputation of the ruler responsible for such conquests. An impersonal cabinet is not likely to be so deeply influenced by this motive; but the glamour of conquest and domination may well inspire an ambitious prince; and most of all in France, where there were old traditions of military glory, and a population which regarded such glory as the highest expression of national genius. But, though the policy of Louis was personal and irresponsible, it was characterized by a very high sense of duty, a paradox explicable only in terms of his unusual psychology; for Louis embodied the state; his reputation was identical with that of the nation; hence all his activities were the inspirations not of Louis the man, but of Louis the personification of France. The one was

the slave of the other; the individual was subjected to the dictates of
an imaginary and semi-corporate self; never for one moment did the
King fail in obedience to the fictitious but domineering personality
which ordered the minutest acts of his life. In no other king was
there such a clearly-marked dualism. But while this enslavement of
the will was responsible for prodigious feats of industry and calculation, it sometimes accounted for a deficiency of normal intelligence;
and the consequence of this defect was to be seen most notably in the
last years of his reign, when he was forced to depend not on himself,
but on his country.

But Louis had another support even more effective than the
ingenuity of himself and his representatives; namely, money. He
was ready to bribe any prince; sometimes, as in England, he found it
expedient to bestow gratuities alternately on the King and the
parliamentary opposition. In Germany, the Electors of Cologne and
Mainz and the Duke of Neuburg were bribed against the Emperor;
after 1670 Bavaria, Osnabrück, and Münster were added to the
tributary states; Denmark, Sweden, and Poland had each to be
bribed; most highly subsidized of all was the Elector of Brandenburg, partly for his alliance or neutrality, partly for his soldiers
and munitions. Between 1669 and 1672 it was mainly by French
money that Louis was able to secure the diplomatic isolation of the
Dutch. The demands on Louis's generosity appear to have increased
in geometric proportion. First a ruler would be bribed; then that
ruler would be more strictly controlled by bribing one or more of
his opponents; then spies would be paid to keep an eye on both sets
of pensionaries; throughout it all, the prices went up, and nobody
seemed willing to support the French interest without being well
paid for doing so. Considering the precautions with which it was
distributed the money produced surprisingly little result. Two of the
most heavily-bribed states, England and Brandenburg, eventually
turned against France; all the money lavished on the Stuarts and
Hohenzollerns proved to be wasted; because bribery which may
influence a dynasty cannot corrupt a race. But it was indeed a great
monarchy which could afford such expenditure.

The twin power of diplomacy was the army. In 1661 France did
not have an organized army; for service was still a matter of personal
bargain between the captain and the recruits whom he enrolled in
virtue of his commission. Pillage made up for the absence of a com-

missariat. With the assistance of Le Tellier and his son Louvois the King steadily built up a highly-organized force. Even these three, however, could not abolish all the abuses in the old system; for commissions might still be bought or granted to favourites; but nevertheless the grades of the army were co-ordinated, and the pursuit of arms was now made a definite career. A professional army was thus created, very different from the old feudal levy. There was at first no difficulty in obtaining recruits, for many joined in order to escape from starvation; but as more and more men were needed in the long wars, deception and force had to be used in order to obtain recruits. Even thus, the reserves of French manhood were not enough for Louis's vast designs, and foreign mercenaries had therefore to be enrolled. Switzerland still supplied such troops; there were English and Scottish regiments in French pay; Savoy and Brandenburg also supplied men. The result was a vast increase in the size of armies—from 70,000 men in 1667 to 270,000 in 1678.

Supreme command was in the King and was shared at his discretion with his brother (*Monsieur*) and the Prince of Condé; until 1675 Louis had also the services of the great Turenne, for whom the special rank of Marshal-General was created. Discipline, strictly enforced on the lower ranks, was not so easily maintained among their superiors; but as the State became more directly the employer, even the highest officers were obliged to sink their personal jealousies in submission to the Crown. At the same time a beginning was made in the training of cadets, and many branches of the service were organized on modern methods; thus, artillery, munitions, commissariat, remount, transport, and hospital services were each placed under the control of responsible commissioners. No longer was it necessary to leave wounded men in the field, or to live by pillage; for campaigns were now preceded by careful administrative preparation.

Most remarkable of all was the development of the science of fortification by Vauban. Sébastien Peprestre de Vauban was born of a poor but noble family in 1633. He served first under Condé in the wars of the Fronde, and was captured by the royalist troops; this led to his introduction to Mazarin, who quickly divined his merit, and employed him to conduct the siege operations of 1658 in the Low Countries. For this he was qualified by genius of a high

order. A mathematician and engineer, he reduced siege and trench
warfare to definite principles, and the success of these principles
was so often demonstrated that Louis preferred this form of warfare
to any other. Vauban had remarkable powers of observation; and
before deciding his method of attack, he made a minute inspection
of the terrain surrounding the besieged fort, sometimes launching
his attack not on the weakest but on the strongest side wherever, by
doing so, he could profit best from natural advantages. In this way
he introduced a scientific element into war; and, in consequence,
most of the military triumphs of the reign were due to his skill.
These included the capture of Douai and Lille in 1667; Maestricht
in 1673; Valenciennes and Cambrai in 1677; Mons in 1691, and
Namur in 1692. Nor did he excel only in attack; for he defended the
frontier by forts at Maubeuge, Longwy, Thionville, Kehl (Strasbourg), and Landau. Unlike his royal master, he thought of
frontiers not only as a means of access to other countries, but as
lines to be defended against invasion; moreover, he knew how
dangerous was the proximity of Paris to the eastern frontier; so he
made an eloquent plea for the construction of adequate defences
round the capital. Almost alone of his contemporaries, he insisted
on the need for security against invasion. By his character and
genius, Vauban takes rank in that high tradition of French general-
ship which includes the names of Carnot and Foch.

These advantages were not at first shared by other states. For
whatever reason, the Protestant nations such as England and Holland were directing their attention to economic expansion rather
than to military glory, and so their contests were as much of the
market as of the battlefield. In contrast, the French were primarily
a martial race, and consequently Louis must have felt a certain
contempt for nations influenced mainly by the quest of profit; in
fact, he may be held to represent an older type of semi-divine
kingship surviving into an age of tradesmen. But the tradesmen,
when roused, proved good soldiers; the Dutch produced William
of Orange; and still worse, England, which was not supposed to be
a military race at all, put Marlborough into the field. These things
could not, however, have been foreseen in 1661, when the Dutch
were quietly monopolizing both herring and spices, or carrying off
French wine and brandy to good markets; and England, still in
dread of the sectaries and old Cromwellian soldiers, could boats

only a few regiments of Guards, and a Militia more interested in parliamentary elections than in any other form of warfare.

Thus, in 1661, when Louis became his own first minister, he was confronted with opportunities such as had never before been presented to a prince. He had acquired by marriage a prospective claim to the rich Spanish inheritance; his cousin in England, not yet securely established, was anxious for a French alliance; his cousin Leopold was accommodating; and most of the princes of Germany were willing to be enrolled among the pensionaries of France. Even more, Louis was assured of the devotion of a great nation, long since disillusioned of political experiment, and now enthusiastic in its devotion to a brilliant monarch. Nor was he deterred by any doubts about his capacity for leadership. He was convinced that justice and morality were on his side; and for his acts he was responsible solely to one whose position seemed not incomparable with his own; namely, to God. It needed only money to make the equipment complete. The money was provided by Colbert.

3
Colbert

In 1661 THE population of France was estimated at about eighteen millions, or more than that of Germany and Austria together, and nearly three times that of England. The land was well able to support its inhabitants; for in climate and soil France is one of the most richly-endowed countries; and though there is no great mineral wealth, yet there is a variety of product sufficient to provide all the necessaries and many of the luxuries of life. This variety is one of the most striking features of France. It is accounted for partly by its geological formations, and partly by its situation between oceanic and continental zones of climate on the one hand and between English Channel and Mediterranean on the other. Thus, Lille is slightly north of Prague and on the same parallel as Kiev; Marseilles is farther south than Florence. Between London and Paris and between Lorraine and Swabia there are marked resemblances of climate; but all these differ in this respect from the mountainous Dauphiné, or the sunny plateaux of Provence, or the drained marshes of La Vendée; for in Dauphiné and many parts of Auvergne the summers are moist, the vegetation is luxuriant, and there is abundance of timber; in Provence, the smaller streams dry up in summer, and conditions are not unlike those prevailing in many parts of Spain and Greece; while in La Vendée and Brittany, the climatic influences are typically oceanic; frosts are of short duration, and conditions favour the growth of fruit and vegetables. In the provinces between Paris and the eastern frontier there is a mingling of the oceanic and continental influences, one result of which is the longer and more sunny autumn, specially favourable to the ripening of the vine; farther south, tobacco can be grown profitably; in the south-west and extreme-west brine can be evaporated to produce salt; and in almost all districts notably in the north and north-east, there are districts of corn, rye, and flax.

Geology has helped to accentuate this diversity. Strata of chalk and clay make possible the growing of cereals to perfection; for example, between Seine and Loire there is the flat corn land of Beauce, dominated by the cathedral of Chartres; elsewhere are to be found some of the heavier clays requisite for pastures and a successful cheese industry; in the Garonne district are numerous lacustrine and fluvial deposits on which can be grown corn and maize, in company with woods and vineyards; in Alsace, there is the deep, black *loess*, one of the most fertile of all soils; in Limagne (Auvergne) is to be found the detritus of old volcanic rock, so rich that cultivation can always be intensive, and the landscape which results is not unlike that of the lower slopes of Vesuvius; in Normandy, the *Pays de Caux* is a land of orchards; in Saintonge and Gascony there are rich alluvial lands producing corn and wine, and on the coast there is salt. Can it be wondered that England fought so strenuously for her possessions in France?

One general result of this conformation is that most districts are specially adapted for what is called *la petite culture*, that is, the cultivation on a small scale of miscellaneous crops, in contrast with large or specialized farming. Apart from mountainous areas such as those of Dauphiné, Auvergne, and the Cevennes the countryside often presents the appearance of shallow valleys and gently-sloping hillsides, produced by the wearing down of river-beds; these slopes, generally called *côtes* or *coteaux*, where they have a southern aspect, are well adapted for the vine, and are to be found notably in the valley of the Moselle, the eastern declivities of the Vosges, and the valleys of the Loire, the Yonne, the Oise, the Charente, and the Saône. In consequence, subsistence cultivation has generally been characteristic of many parts of France; and this has been accentuated by the fact that, unlike their English compeers, the greater French nobility were frequently non-resident and few of them were even interested in agriculture. In England, on the other hand, men who had made money in the town generally founded noble families which resided in the country; consequently there was a continuous flow of surplus wealth from town to country; but there was little of this process in France, where landlords exercised their rights, but rarely lent the aid of either their capital or encouragement. Consequently, the peasant was left to fight his own battles; and the soil of France was cultivated by men and women who, if they were stolid and unenterprising were invariably frugal and hard-working; they were often gross and ignorant, but they were attached to their holdings with that almost fierce devotion which can be seen even today in *la terre qui meurt*. Hence also a lower standard of life in the French countryside, most clearly evidenced by the comparatively small proportion of wheat in the bread.

Thus France at the accession of Louis XIV had most of the human and natural resources requisite for national prosperity and peace. Frenchmen were not a sparse population of survivors trying to cultivate a desert as were most of the people of Germany; they were more fortunate in climate and soil than were the Spaniards; they were not so divided by religious differences as were Englishmen. They had no mercantile marine such as the Dutch possessed, but there were enormous forests which, if properly developed, could supply timber for the building of great fleets; trade was active in the weaving and cloth-making towns and villages; a silk industry was centred in Lyon; canvas was made in the Breton villages, and this, with the brandy of the Charente and the salt of the south-west, was a profitable article of export. There were increasing imports and re-exports of sugar from the colonies in the west; from Marseilles and Toulon there was an old trading connexion with the Levant and Syria; every spring, fleets of Breton and Norman fishermen left for the fishing stations of Newfoundland. It needed only organization and encouragement to develop the latent wealth of France.

The death of Mazarin left Louis free to act as his own first minister, and for more than half a century thereafter the history of France is stamped with the impression of his will. That will was exercised through the medium of councillors and ministers. Of the ministers there were six—the Chancellor, the Controller-General of Finance, and the four Secretaries of State. The Chancellor was head of the whole judicial system and was the highest officer of State. The Controller-General of Finance, originally a subordinate official, became of supreme importance after the disgrace of Fouquet (1664); for the Controller-General was the nearest equivalent to the English Lord High Treasurer; and as finance became more essential in the shaping of policy, the purse-bearer came to exercise functions not unlike those of a first minister. But his duties were never completely specialized; because in addition to his general control over government expenditure, he frequently interfered with other departments, such as artillery and munitions, communications and public works. The four Secretaries of State were allocated respectively to the Royal Household, War, Foreign Affairs, and the Navy. Originally, the secretaries had been clerks, responsible only for correspondence with each of the four administrative divisions of France; they were now heads of departments, but something of the old geographical distribution still survived, and in practice their duties overlapped in a most complicated manner. Thus, each was still accountable for the administration of one of the four geographical divisions; the Secretary of Foreign Affairs had the bureau of pensions; his colleague of the Royal Household supervised ecclesiastical affairs; moreover, a secretary might at any moment be transferred to the duties of another; or one man might have to perform the work of two secretaryships, as did Colbert, who, after 1666, was also Controller-General of Finance.

The consequence was that, for a capable and energetic minister there were unlimited opportunities for acquiring an expert knowledge of the working of the government machine, since he was unlikely to be bound down to one set of duties throughout his career; on the other hand, the multiplicity and diversity of these functions might so overwhelm a mediocre or incompetent man that he would be reduced to impotence. In other words, France had reached that point of evolution when the expert was needed; but there were no facilities for training or selecting the expert. Nor was the King completely free to choose his ministers, because an outgoing secretary might expect a large sum from his successor, and to this extent choice was limited to those able to pay the price. Moreover, Louis's best servants were not chosen by him, but were left to him by Mazarin; and on their deaths they were replaced not by ministers, but by courtiers, a change clearly reflected in the last two decades of the reign.

Of the councils, the most important was the Royal Council or Council of State (*Conseil du Roi* or *Conseil d'État*), which was subdivided into sections according as it dealt with policy, legislation, or supreme administration. Thus, one section, the Cabinet Council (*Conseil d'en haut*), considered supreme matters of government;

it met only when convened by the King, who might limit his confidence to a portion of it, or might keep his own counsels; this cabinet included only ministers. The Council of Despatches (*Conseil des Dépêches*), another branch of the Royal Council, dealt with correspondence from the provinces, and exercised a censorship over books; the Council of Finance (*Conseil des Finances*) adjudicated on disputes between the Treasury and the tax-payers; the Privy Council (*Conseil Privé*) was a supreme court of appeal from all inferior tribunals, and was presided over by the Chancellor.

Such were the chief central institutions of the executive. The link between them and the provinces was not the provincial governor, but the intendant, a comparatively new class of official, whose powers had been revived and extended by Richelieu. There was one intendant for each of the thirty-four *generalities* into which the country was divided. Many questions of administration and judicature were settled on the spot by these men, whose powers were almost unlimited in extent; for they had a general supervision over agriculture, industry, and education; they saw that repairs to highways and bridges were effected; they had a large measure of control over the municipalities in their generality; they assisted the tax collectors, and adjudicated wherever there was a conflict of jurisdictions; they kept the executive fully informed of all that was going on within their province; they were billeting officers, police superintendents, sanitary inspectors, and rate collectors; they could order a man to do a thing and imprison him if he refused; in sum they were the human agents who kept this vast machine working. They might be compared with the English justices of the peace, but for the fact that the scope of their powers was so much wider; also they were paid, and they were sometimes spies; for they might report unfavourably on the conduct of a local Parlement, or send accounts of speeches made by deputies in the local Estates. They represented not the province, but the Government; and they decided on their own initiative many matters which in England would have had to be taken to the law courts.

A glance at the correspondence from intendants will reveal something of their functions. Thus, an intendant writing from Languedoc informs his superiors in Paris that several deputies of the Third Estate are complaining about the *gabelle*; a colleague in Dauphiné writes that the harvest is expected to be good, and therefore the question of permitting the export of corn will have to be considered; the official in Caen sends a memoir on the inequalities of the *taille*; from Auvergne there is a complaint of the increase of municipal debts, and a protest against the excessive number of exemptions from taxation; out of Hainault comes an account of murders and robberies committed by the Spanish soldiers, and the difficulty of enforcing justice, because there are no towns, but only walled villages; the intendant of Provence states that the harvest is poor and not enough to permit export; his colleague of Berry has a sad tale of bad harvests and deaths among the cattle, which provide the chief industry of the province; from Montauban the question is raised how far the River Lot can be considered navigable, a problem to be determined not locally but in Paris; the functionary in Orléans complains that, since the Parisian operatives have been given permission to make all sorts of stockings, the stocking industry of Orléans has fallen away to nothing; from Evreux is an announcement that the bishop has refused to allow his clergy to make a contribution towards defraying the debt of the municipality, so there will be required an order of the Council to bring him to a sense of his duty; the intendant in La Rochelle writes about the bad winter, and the need for funds to provide roads through the marshes. Such is an infinitesimal portion of the correspondence which passed between these officials and the central executive.

Even this tiny selection reveals one characteristic difficulty experienced by the intendants—that of preventing the municipalities from falling into debt. It was this fact which enabled Louis's Government to exercise a stricter control over these local corporations, until eventually they lost their autonomy. Meanwhile, the close and often corrupt oligarchies ruling these corporations were generally willing to pay money in order to retain their immunities and privileges; this is why they often proved serious impediments to both enterprising ministers and efficient intendants; for everywhere reform might be thwarted by provincialism and prescription, or stifled by the indifference or corruption of the Court. In these circumstances the system could work with success only if controlled by a superman. The superman was Colbert.

Jean Baptiste Colbert was born at Rheims in 1610, the son of a merchant draper; he was educated for a lawyer, and had some training as a banker. These facts have each a special significance.

That the son of a *bourgeois* should attain to supreme office in the administration was a novelty; for hitherto such posts had been confined almost exclusively to men of birth; indeed, Colbert's family was so conscious of this phenomenon that they laboured to prove their kinship with the Northumbrian Saint Cuthbert; and, at some expense, they at last succeeded in procuring a complete family tree which established their distinguished ancestry. From his *bourgeois* birth Colbert brought the characteristics of industry, parsimony, zeal for detail, love of order, and routine; to these he added organizing and driving power. These qualities were supplemented by aptitudes derived from legal education and business training. In France, to study law did not mean frequenting one of the Inns of Court to learn the art of forensic debate; it implied a more definitely professional equipment, and as Roman Law was generally included, the student was familiarized with codes and the science of codification. Colbert learned from his legal studies how to draft a code. Banking gave him some knowledge of finance, currency, and exchange, as well as an appreciation of the utility of credit. His energy urged him to find out things for himself; his insight showed what should be done; and his juristic training enabled him to draft his reforms.

There was little of the idealist in his composition. He believed in wealth as the source of power; and he insisted that everyone in the State should contribute to the sum total of that wealth. Hence he condemned the multiplicity of priests and monks, he was severe on idlers; he admired England and Holland, where merchants were held in repute, and policy was directed to the promotion of trade and industry. He knew and deplored the ingrained French love for the 'black-coat' professions; he regretted also the inequalities of taxation, and the great diversity of weights and measures throughout France; these, he thought, should be unified and standardized. The State, with the help of her colonies, should be homogeneous, disciplined, and self-supporting, exporting her products and manufactured goods in her own ships, and defending them with her fleets. With these views Colbert was, to some extent, out of place; for France was still an agricultural, not an industrial country, dependent mainly on cereals and the culture of the vine, and dominated by religious and militarist aspirations, both fittingly embodied in Colbert's master Louis. But in at least one respect

Colbert shared the prepossessions of his time. He believed that international trade was a form of warfare; that the triumph of one country must inevitably be at the expense of another; that wealth was measured by bullion; that tariffs, aggression, and conquest are the best means of accumulating and monopolizing bullion, and are therefore of necessity the weapons by which national greatness is achieved.

Colbert entered the service of Le Tellier, Secretary of State for War, in 1648, in which service he so distinguished himself that he was taken into the confidence of Mazarin, and recommended by that astute observer of men to the good graces of Louis. An opportunity for promotion soon occurred. Fouquet, the *surintendant général des finances*, was dishonest, but with such public notoriety that a special tribunal was erected to try him; and Colbert worked hard at the task of collecting evidence against the man who stood in his way. For nearly four years the trial proceeded, lengthened out by long speeches in which the accused financier generally succeeded in evading the specific charges. His defence was really an indictment of the whole financial system; for he showed how even an honest minister must be at the mercy of the Court. He was eventually found guilty (1664) and imprisoned in the fortress of Pignerol (Piedmont), a fortress then in French possession; but before the end of the trial most of his powers were being exercised by Colbert. The old office of Superintendent-General of Finance was abolished; nevertheless, as Controller-General the new minister wielded most of his prerogatives. He was not much more honest than his disgraced predecessor; indeed, in this connexion honesty is a relative term, but he did not make a great display; he was abstemious and undemonstrative, so his wealth did not excite public envy. From his cold demeanour he was named *The North*. In 1669 he combined his financial duties with two secretaryships—those of the Navy and the Royal Household; he also founded one of the great ministerial families of the reign; for his son Seignelai succeeded him as Secretary for the Navy, his younger brother, Colbert de Croissi, was a diplomatist, and his nephew Torcy was a distinguished Secretary for Foreign Affairs. The rival family was that of Louvois, the Secretary for War, who was the son of Le Tellier and the father of Barbezieux. Colbert and Louvois represented the rival policies between which Louis at first hesitated; the one for commercial expansion and development of

navy and mercantile marine; the other for concentration on the
army and the achievement of military glory. Louis chose the latter.

Colbert's administration may be considered according as it
concerned, first, finance and taxation; secondly, agriculture,
commerce, and industry; and finally, colonies, the navy, and
mercantile marine.

The special tribunal which found Fouquet guilty investigated
the whole financial system and condemned thousands of malver-
sators to make restitution; but, as generally happened when such
commissions attempted to effect a clearance, the smaller fry alone
were penalized, and the wealthier speculators were able to secure
immunity by bribes. Nevertheless, this investigation showed Colbert
what were the most serious abuses; namely, the uneconomic nature
of the *taille*, and the dependance of the Government on tax-farmers,
most of them in alliance with the Court. Had the minister had a
free hand he would have effected radical reforms; but, like so many
reformers, he soon realized that, to a large extent, he was at the
mercy of the system which he would have changed. Finding the
administration saddled with a large debt, and the revenue from
Crown lands greatly diminished by alienations and usurpations,
he first set himself to the task of bringing back alienated rights, and
introducing some order into the conduct of the finances. Like Sully
before him, he insisted on accurate book-keeping and accountancy.
Perquisites were reduced to moderate dimensions; stricter bargains
were made with the tax-farmers; all the alienated Crown rights were
carefully investigated and defective titles were set aside. One of his
objects was to make the *taille* uniform by levying it solely on landed
property; but he was unable to effect this reform, and had to content himself with reducing its rate, at the cost of a diminished yield.
The deficiency was made good by an increase in the taxes known as
the *aides*, which fell mainly on wine, and were therefore borne by a
larger portion of the community. In the internal Customs he
succeeded in effecting this reform, that these dues were unified in
the central areas known as the *Cinq Grosses Fermes*; outside this
area, however, the old diversity and multiplicity remained. By
better management, and in consequence of the increased national
wealth directly due to his reforms, Colbert succeeded in obtaining
greatly increased revenues, an improvement which did not continue
for long after 1672, when Louis embarked on the war with Holland;

and so Colbert was eventually obliged to acquiesce in more abnormal methods of raising money.

In fiscal policy, therefore, he had to utilize the materials at hand; he could attempt no far-reaching change; but he tried to eliminate the worst evils of the system. Early in his administration he directed attention to the *Rentes*. At first he was anxious to suppress them; accordingly, some were paid off, others were compounded for, and many holdings were repudiated altogether; the remaining lots were then grouped in a conversion scheme, the rate of interest being reduced from $5\frac{1}{2}$ per cent. to 5 per cent. Like Louis, he would willingly have dispensed altogether with *Rentes* as a means of raising capital; but here again he had little choice, and by 1672 he was obliged to resort once more to the *bourgeois* lenders. He offered $5\frac{1}{2}$ per cent., but the response was poor; and even when he raised it to $6\frac{1}{2}$ per cent. he found a natural unwillingness to lend money to the State. Nevertheless, in spite of his preference for tax to loan, he decided to profit by an example set in England, where, for a brief period prior to its stop in 1672, the Exchequer had served some of the purposes of a national bank; an achievement due to the application of two principles, first, the allocation of security to definite funds, and repayment of loans from private persons in strict chronological sequence, without interruption from either favour or importunity. The English experiment had proved short-lived, but Colbert did not see why it should not succeed in France.

Accordingly, in 1674 he set up a national loan office (*caisse des emprunts*) in which he proceeded to administer the *Rentes*. The novelty in this scheme was that for the first time in France the State offered definite guarantees for repayment; these being, first, assignment of the security on a definite tax, namely, a portion of the internal Customs; secondly, an undertaking to pay 5 per cent. and to refund the loans in strict sequence. A written receipt was given, and it was clearly Colbert's intention, by the revival of confidence among the *rentiers*, to obtain from them, as cheaply as possible, short-term loans. This was one of his most notable achievements; but, though successful, it did not long survive its originator; for in 1684 Louis ordered these funds to be paid off, and, in place of the *bourgeois* investors, the speculators, with their long-term loans on exorbitant terms, again came into their own. Thus Colbert very nearly succeeded in creating a system of national credit, which might well have had momentous consequences on the later history of France; but this, like so many of his reforms, perished with his death. Louis never forgot and never forgave; to him, the word *rentier* meant sedition and the Fronde.

If Colbert was able to make little impression on the fiscal system of the Ancien Régime he was yet able so to develop the natural resources of France as to effect a great increase in the national revenue, even with the wasteful and unjust taxes which supplied that revenue. His official duties gave him a minute knowledge of every sphere of national enterprise; from the intendants he could obtain information about local conditions and their suitability for new experiments; and by the collation of statistics and information he was enabled to create a public intelligence bureau qualified to give advice on crops and manufactures. His services to agriculture may first be noted. He was not convinced that viticulture was the enterprise best adapted for his countrymen; for he was of the industrial north, and somewhat hostile to the wine-growing departments; he therefore did nothing to encourage the culture of the vine. In its place he preferred crops such as hemp and flax, since these were the bases of useful industries; he tried also to promote the culture of madder and woad in order to provide dyes. Horse-breeding he encouraged in order that France might be independent of foreign supplies; this was specially successful in Normandy and Poitou. He permitted the export of corn when harvests were good; but he could not completely break down the barriers of internal Customs which prevented the transport of wheat from one province to another; in consequence there might be abundance in one province and famine in another. Having none of the knowledge of husbandry and husbandmen which can be acquired only by life in the country, he rendered only mediocre services to agriculture. He had more faith in commerce and industry.

In these spheres he was at his best. Industries were regulated in a carefully co-ordinated scheme; size, quality, and design being carefully prescribed in numerous edicts; in this way he took over from the corporations their exclusive control of industry and vested it in the State. His regulations entailed a greater sub-division of labour, and so a cheapening in the cost of production; in many enterprises a factory system was introduced. In these factories a semi-monastic discipline prevailed; for the conduct of the worker was kept

under strict surveillance; he must not swear, nor speak irreverently
of religious things; on Sundays and Holy Days he had to attend
divine service; if he must sing at work, he had to confine himself
to sacred chants, and in such a low voice that his neighbours were
not disturbed. This was Colbert's only concession to the monastic
ideal. Not only did he provide for separate industries, but he
arranged them all in a hierarchy headed by the workshops of the
Gobelins, a royal manufactory which specialized in furniture,
tapestry, statuary, gold- and silver-ware; the workmanship being
under the general supervision of the artist Le Brun. The workmen
of the Gobelins were paid by the State, and attached to the work-
shop was a school for the training of sixty apprentices. Then there
were over one hundred manufactories of which the King was
'protector'; on these the title 'royal' was conferred, and they included the manufactures of cloth, silk, linen, and lace in addition to
tapestry and furniture. Special privileges were conferred on these
'royal' industries: their patentees might bear the fleur-de-lis; their
workmen were exempted from the *taille*; the nobility might engage
therein without loss of status; they were encouraged by subsidies.
But these advantages were liable to be abused; for men sometimes
obtained them in order to procure a loan, or to defeat a rival.

Throughout France the textile industries were committed to such
companies; and in those places where no industries were already in
existence, attempts were made to grow flax or dyeing stuffs so that
there might be raw material on which men, women, and children
could be set to work. New plantations of mulberry trees were
planted for the culture of the silk worm, and the city of Lyon became
the rich centre of an improved silk industry; farther north was the
lace factory at Auxerre, where the children of the poor were encouraged and sometimes obliged to serve an apprenticeship.
Equally with the textile crafts the metal and mining industries
were fostered. Colbert visualized a France where everyone was at
work; no paupers, no monks, no nuns; no pilgrimages, and as few
saints' days as possible. A host of inspectors ensured conformity with
the multitudinous rules and specifications; and in his Ordinance
of Commerce (1673) the minister formulated his rules for apprenticeship, contracts, and foreign trade in a comprehensive code which
remained in force until the Revolution.

Nor was he dependent solely on French workmen. A Florentine

named Bellinzani was appointed to superintend the inspectors; Swedish and German miners were introduced in order to teach improved methods of mining and smelting; Venetian glass-blowers were brought to Paris that they might teach the mysteries of their craft; the women of Burano came to instruct in the making of lace. There were also foreign capitalists and large-scale employers such as the Dutch van Robais at Abbeville, who employed many of the population in the making of linen. Colbert believed that by administrative control and encouragement all these industries could be acclimatized in France; just as he thought that, in obedience to his decrees, the women of Auxerre would willingly change from the domestic to the factory system. But it is possible that he confided too much in the efficacy of regulations; and it is clear that after his death little more than his codes remained. Colbert could galvanize France into activity; he created a glow of life in a moribund state; but it needed almost superhuman energy, and as soon as the man was gone the old torpor returned.

The Controller-General was convinced of the importance of good internal communications, and that France was at a disadvantage as compared with Holland because the canals were undeveloped, and produce had to be conveyed on bad roads. So he effected improvements in highways and bridges, and he completed the first paved road between Paris and Orléans; he also encouraged the engineers Riquet and Vauban to construct the canal from the Garonne to the Aude, connecting Bordeaux with Toulouse and linking the Atlantic with the Mediterranean. This waterway, finished in 1681, was nearly 170 miles in length, and it was hoped that foreign shipping would take advantage of the shorter sea-passage which it provided; but this hope was never realized, for the Canal of the Two Seas was used for little more than local traffic. France did not have really good means of communication until the administration of Orry (1730–45). Colbert's influence is to be seen also in the streets and quays of Paris, many of which he widened; he was also active in the intellectual life of the capital; a patron of science, letters, and art; an active spirit in the foundation of the Observatory, and the Academies of Inscriptions, Science, Architecture, Painting, and Sculpture. He should be judged not by his failures, many of which were inevitable, but by the vision, energy, and intellectual order which he brought to bear on the herculean tasks imposed upon him.

His activities may be traced also in colonization and the development of the fleets. One of his objects was to make France a great colonial power. In North America she possessed Arcadia, several ports in Newfoundland, and territories on Hudson's Bay; farther south, stretching far into the interior, was Louisiana. These possessions gave France a unique strategic position in the west for, by their geographical disposition, she had control over the Saint Lawrence and Mississippi and had free access to the great lakes; while, in contrast, the English settlements on the coast were wedged in between the great river mouths, and progress into the interior was hampered by the Alleghenies. In the West Indies France possessed a number of important islands, including Martinique, Guadeloupe, and a part of St. Kitts; in South America there was a settlement in Guiana; in Africa were the stations of Senegal for the slave trade, and Madagascar was wholly French. In India her influence was strong in Ceylon; also in Chandernagore, Pondicherry, and Masulipatam; indeed, in 1661 it might have been thought that France was the power of the future in India. Considering her population, her resources, and her possessions east and west, France, in the opinion of Colbert, was well fitted to take part in the race for colonial and maritime supremacy.

There was general agreement in western Europe that colonies should be exploited solely for the benefit of the mother country, and that as far as possible the foreigner should be excluded from trade with them. England had already inaugurated her policy of the Navigation Acts; Spain closed her colonial empire to foreigners; the Dutch kept out every competitor from the East India spice islands, and attempted to enforce the same policy on the west coast of Africa; the Portuguese were obliged to give away parts of their empire in order to procure support against Spain. Many of the French possessions overseas were on a proprietary basis; and so long as there was a private element in their ownership, it was difficult or impossible to impose on them a regular system. So in 1664 Colbert began his policy of buying out these proprietary rights and administering the colonial possessions through monopolist companies directly responsible to the Crown; in that year two such companies were founded—that of the West Indies and that of the East Indies; the first having its offices and docks at Havre, the second at Lorient. Later was founded the Levant Company, which had factories in the eastern Mediterranean and an agent at Constantinople; because of the shorter sea passage from Marseilles or Toulon this company was able to compete on very favourable terms with the English Levant Company. The Northern Company was founded for trade with the Baltic ports. These companies illustrate many of the standard principles and prejudices entertained regarding colonies; namely, restriction of trade with them to privileged nationals; export thereto of native products and manufactures, and the import therefrom of raw material, notably sugar, tobacco, spice, and cotton. Colonial and commercial policy were thus inseparable; the monopolist trading company was the link between the home country and the overseas possession; it was also an agent of government, for the East India and West India Companies had powers of civil and military jurisdiction in the territories allotted to them. Elsewhere French influence was maintained by consuls and diplomatic agents.

Most of these companies came to an end in Colbert's lifetime, not because they were failures, but because they had achieved their purpose of consolidating French control. Once this was established, it was possible to dissolve the company and throw the trade open to French merchants. In order to illustrate the strength and weakness of Colbert as a minister of colonial affairs, special reference may be made to the work of his West India Company.

The French West Indies clearly demonstrated the Dutch preponderance in the carrying trade; for there the Hollander lent money to needy planters and exported their products; thereby securing freights and a return on investment. By the establishment of the West India Company Colbert set himself to the task of ending this state of affairs. The Company was assigned a wide sphere of activity—all the possessions in South America, the French West Indies, Newfoundland, Acadia, and Canada; the old proprietors were compensated, and a strict monopoly was enforced. The funds necessary for the activities of the Company were raised by subscription. By 1674, when the Company was dissolved, the minister had succeeded in his main object—to keep the French West Indies for the French; and by that time there had developed a prosperous trade in sugar, carried in French ships. In 1662 only four such ships had been engaged in this trade; by 1683 the number was more than two hundred. Concurrently with this occurred a great development of the ports of Bordeaux, La Rochelle, and Nantes, and thus France became a serious rival to both England and Holland in the world's carrying trade. Moreover, the colonies provided a good market for French exports, which consisted mainly of wine, brandy, olive oil, cloth; with Irish salt-beef and butter (from an Irish community at Nantes); in consequence of increased imports of raw sugar, many refineries were started, and France became one of the European staples for the supply of raw sugar. What Canada and the West Indies meant to French prosperity at this time may be visualized by inspecting the fallen greatness of ports such as Nantes and La Rochelle, and comparing them with Glasgow and Liverpool which, in the seventeenth century, had only a few thousand tons of shipping between them. But for France's continental entanglements Canada might still have been French, and Bristol might long have remained the greatest of British western ports.

In general, Colbert's colonial policy was both enlightened and successful. But even here some of his limitations can be detected. Thus, he did not derive much advantage from tobacco imports, because this commodity was a monopoly, granted to a syndicate which controlled the market in both the French and colonial product. It was in consequence of manipulation by this 'ring' that little tobacco was re-exported. Nor did France profit fully from her expanding sugar trade, mainly because of Colbert's obtuse policy in regard to the by-products, of which the two most important are rum and molasses. The French planters were anxious to dispose of these; but Colbert would not allow them to send their rum to France, lest it might compete with the native brandy; nor would he allow them to trade their molasses with New England, in spite of the willingness of the New England colonies to barter it in exchange for their provisions and manufactured goods. Colbert insisted on keeping out the foreigner altogether, even at the expense of impoverishing the planters; and so French colonial enterprise suffered from a certain lack of elasticity. But it would be wrong to condemn the minister on this account; for he was acting on the currently-accepted principles of his time.

In attempting to make his country a great colonial power Colbert was setting himself against some of the most deeply engrained prejudices of his contemporaries. His countrymen produced many great pioneers and explorers; but, on the other hand, the average Frenchman had little inclination to try his fortune in the new world, and so the colonies, including Canada, suffered from a lack of population. More serious, Colbert had to contend with, and never quite overcame, the social prejudice against commerce, trade, and emigration; for the French nobility was not only indifferent to these things, but actually hostile; and it should be recalled that then more than now the upper classes exerted a determining influence on national life and opinion. Still more serious, Louis was not convinced of the importance of colonial and maritime expansion. He listened with patience to the wearisome reports of his minister; he paid generous subscriptions to the new colonial companies; but he regarded these things as of secondary interest, and valued trade in proportion as it supplied the sinews of war; it was an ignoble means to a good end. On the other side of the Channel was Charles II, indifferent to everything but his pleasure; willing, in return for money, to keep England out of European entanglements; doubtless a sordid and ignoble policy, but at least affording his subjects the opportunity to develop in peace their colonies and trade. Bombay and Calcutta, New York and New Jersey; the Carolinas and Pennsylvania; these were among the concrete achievements of English enterprise, obtained by a minimum of military effort; whereas Louis consumed enormous armies in the acquisition of towns and villages, many of which had eventually to be surrendered. His European aggressions were necessarily at the expense of empire.

The development of the navy and mercantile marine were essential parts of Colbert's colonial policy. For this, the first requisite was a supply of timber. In his Ordinance of Waters and Forests (1669) Colbert enunciated the principles of a national timber policy, and by his improved administration of the forests he made France independent of supplies from the Baltic. At the same time he subsidized shipbuilding; with the result that there was a great increase of French tonnage. On this basis he strengthened the navy, so that by 1677 it was comparable in size with those of England and Holland; for in that year it consisted of 116 ships, 12 being first-rates and 26 second-rates. After it was taken over from England, Dunkirk was strongly fortified; a new naval arsenal was created at Rochefort on the Charente, thus providing a possible substitute for the Huguenot La Rochelle; Toulon and Brest became great naval dockyards. At Rochefort and Toulon naval hospitals were established. Marseilles remained the headquarters of the Mediterranean galley fleets, the crews of which were composed of French convicts, Turkish slaves, negroes, and (after 1685), Protestants; but elsewhere the navy comprised ships of more modern design, manned by expert crews. In place of the old press gang Colbert introduced in the ports a system of maritime conscription; but this had to be enforced by penalties; and France, like England, suffered from the harsh and unjust methods employed in obtaining naval crews. It was even more difficult to secure competent naval officers. There were, it is true, training ships at Rochefort and Brest, and the Newfoundland fleets supplied qualified seamen; but the higher commands were still filled by men promoted from land service, or chosen on account of their birth. These were socially distinguished on board ship by their uniform and privileges from officers who had risen from sea service; with the result that there were constant disputes and duels, and efficiency suffered. In the English navy a similar contrast divided the 'gentleman' from the 'tarpaulin' officer; indeed, the Dutch were the only nation which did not regard a training in the mercanile marine as a social stigma. Hence two entirely different and even antagonistic classes of naval officer; D'Estrées representing the type of French admiral qualified only by birth or military exploits, Duquesne and Tourville the newer type, trained at sea and promoted after distinguished service.

In the strengthening of navy and mercantile marine is to be found the most permanent achievement of Colbert. By encouraging the native supply of timber, hemp, tar, and canvas and by subsidies to builders he created tonnage; by his system of maritime conscription he brought into existence a reserve of about 50,000 trained men. He founded a school of naval gunnery; and by promoting the study of hydrography he made possible the production of more accurate charts. He established regiments of Marines; but characteristically these were afterwards transferred to land service. Colbert proved how, by skilled direction and encouragement, a nation not hitherto distinguished for maritime achievement might be so trained as to become a serious competitor with nations more definitely dependent on the sea and more habituated to maritime enterprise. That France had available good human material for navy and mercantile marine was proved then as it has been proved since.

Such in brief were the main reforms of Colbert. They made possible the public activities of Louis XIV.

4

Louis the Dictator of Europe, 1661–78

IT WAS NOT long before Europe experienced the steadily growing power of Louis XIV. A scuffle for precedence between the Spanish and French ambassadors in London (1661) was followed by the enforced withdrawal of the former and the humiliation of Spain; in Rome, the French ambassador was the indirect cause of another riot, when his servants came into conflict with the Pope's Corsican Guard. This was followed by a siege of the French embassy, and the ejection of the ambassador's wife from her carriage. Louis demanded full retribution, failing which he would annex Avignon; to this threat Pope Alexander VII yielded, and even consented to the erection of a pyramid commemorating his disgrace and submission. The pyramid would have been a curious memorial in the head-quarters of Christendom; and Louis, with his genius for detail, actively concerned himself with its design, insisting that the inscription thereon should be in letters of such size that they might easily be read by a spectator. Fortunately, however, the Pope found a means of evading the stipulation, and within a short time this unusual piece of masonry was removed. More honourable were French activities in the Mediterranean against the Barbary Corsairs, and the sending of a French expeditionary force to Austria for service with the Imperial Army against the Turks; this contingent distinguished itself at the battle of St. Gothard in August 1664.

Meanwhile there was a notable addition to French territory by the purchase of Dunkirk from Charles II (October 1662), and at the same time a treaty was signed with the Duke of Lorraine whereby the duke granted the reversion of his duchy to Louis, on condition that he retained a life interest. The treaty was never ratified, owing to difficulties about the precedence to be accorded to Duke Charles among the French nobility; but the negotiations provided at least a pretext for further intervention in Lorraine, as Louis now regarded himself as its duke. He did not succeed however in obtaining from Spain a formal cancellation of his wife's surrender of her 'claim' to the Spanish Succession; but on the other hand, by the marriage of the English King with the Infanta of Portugal he obtained a potential ally against Spain; and he furnished Charles with sub-sidies to be spent in providing military help to Portugal. So long as his father-in-law Philip IV lived, Louis would not publicly ally with the Portuguese in their struggle for independence; but secretly he was promoting this end by financial assistance to Portugal's public ally, England. A similar process was at work in Germany, where several princes 'commended' themselves to the French overlord; and in 1664 the Elector of Brandenburg renewed his alliance. Sweden and Denmark were also enrolled among Louis's confederates; of greater consequence was an offensive and defensive alliance with the Dutch, signed in April 1662. This alliance promised to be of service to Louis whenever he commenced operations in the Spanish Netherlands; and to the Dutch, if their commercial disputes with England led to war. So, before Philip IV died (1665) his country was practically isolated in a Europe which was beginning to recognize the hegemony of France.

These were years of peace, but precarious peace. The first Anglo-Dutch War (1652–4) had not settled the question of maritime supremacy, contested by English and Dutch; already the two races were coming to blows in the East Indies and on the West Coast of Africa; unsettled disputes between their merchants caused a steady accumulation of claims by one nation against the other. Early in 1664 an English force seized New Netherlands, which became the colonial province of New York. Then followed the Second Anglo-Dutch War (1665–7); one more unsuccessful attempt to determine which of the two powers was to be supreme at sea. This war dis-turbed the natural evolution of Louis's schemes. On the one hand, it was in his interests that the two mercantile races should weaken themselves by conflict; but on the other hand there was the treaty of 1662 by which he was bound to assist the Dutch. For long he hesit-ated; and before hostilities were declared he tried to induce Charles to come to terms; but the war was popular in England, and Charles went the way of his people. During the first year of the war the Dutch suffered some reverses at sea; and it became more obvious that, if he wished to maintain his reputation, Louis would have to join the fray. So he kept his word; and early in 1666 he declared war on England.

His conduct now showed a curious compromise. Secretly he was the friend of the English king and wished to transform this friendship into an alliance; publicly he was the ally of Holland, but in reality he was beginning to dislike the Dutch. So he sent ships to the West Indies to attack the English colonies; there he secured some successes until an English fleet arrived and reversed them; but in European waters he did not send a single ship to the help of his ally. Such a compromise is understandable; but it assumed an unusual form in Louis's mind. He wrote to Charles, emphasizing how little he had done for the Dutch; he confided that his declaration of war on England was only a 'scrap of parchment'; and even before the end of the war (July 1667) he signed a treaty with his public enemy the English king by which both monarchs undertook, for one year, not to enter into any alliance against the other. With the Dutch, on the other hand, Louis expatiated on the great sacrifices he had made by keeping his word to them. It would be carping to call this hypocrisy; for he appears to have convinced himself that he was 'a martyr to his word', the consolatory phrase applied to him by Charles of England.

Another event helped to clarify the issues. This was the death of Philip IV in September 1665, at the moment when the Portuguese had practically won their independence. By his will, Philip definitely excluded Maria Theresa from the succession; and provided that, in the event of his son Charles having no male heir, the inheritance should go to his younger daughter Margaret, who had married the Emperor Leopold. Here was an official pronouncement completely destroying the dormant claims which French diplomacy had so assiduously laboured to bring to life. But the machinery which Louis controlled was ready for this emergency; and already it had accumulated much historical fuel for the new demands about to be made on it. For some time Louis's agents had been busy collecting information about the customs regulating the inheritance of private property in the Low Countries. In certain districts it was found that such property 'devolved' on daughters by a first marriage in preference to sons by a second; in some there was an equal partition among all the children; in others all the children succeeded, the sons taking twice as much as the daughters. These customs related only to private property; and were quite distinct from and contrary to the principles governing the descent of the territories wherein these private customs prevailed. Indeed, if all or any of the rules regulating succession to private estates could be used to justify claims to sovereignty, then Europe would be reduced to chaos; for most of the rulers were interrelated, and from these supposed 'rights' of their wives, mothers, and daughters they could have claimed territory everywhere.

But just as Louis persuaded himself that the Dutch were heavily in his debt because he had kept his word with them; so he was convinced that these Flemish territories, or at least portions of them, were French in right of his wife. He formulated his claims publicly in a *Treatise of the rights of the Most Christian Queen*; and an astonished Europe was asked to endorse their justice; nor was a reasonable time given in which to investigate them; for in May 1667 before the Anglo-Dutch War was ended, Louis sent Turenne with 35,000 troops into the Low Countries. Within a few months Charleroi, Courtrai, Douai, and Lille were captured. Thus, before the end of the Second Anglo-Dutch War (in which he was nominally a participant) Louis cut across it with an invasion, the object of which was to obtain the Spanish Netherlands. Unlike the later invasions, this had a consistent and to some extent justifiable motive; and its speedy execution would have done much to simplify the question of the frontier; indeed, the historians who applaud Frederick the Great's acquisition of Silesia, could have found even more justification for Louis's design on Flanders, *if he had carried it out.*

He was speedily faced by a coalition of powers dismayed by this threat to European stability. In January 1668 was signed by the representatives of England, Holland, and Sweden the celebrated Triple Alliance, the declared object of which was to reduce France to her frontiers as determined by the Treaty of the Pyrenees. Thus Charles of England had definitely broken his word, given less than a year before; the Dutch, it is true, were also among those who declared against Louis, but in doing so they were not violating any definite agreement. Louis's reply was prompt. In February 1668

Condé invaded Franche Comté and captured the whole province for his master. Thus was demonstrated the overwhelming superiority of French arms. That it was no more than a demonstration may be inferred from the fact that in January 1668 Louis had signed with the Emperor Leopold a treaty dividing the Spanish Empire between them; on the principle that the Emperor was to have Spain, the West Indies, and the Balearic Islands; while France was to have her 'devolution' possessions in the Low Countries, together with Franche Comté or Luxembourg. In the (likely) event of Charles of Spain dying without a male heir, France was to have the whole of Flanders, with Naples, Sicily, and the North African possessions. This partition was to be completed on the death of Charles II of Spain; a child of such prodigiously bad health that his death was expected very soon.

Thus in the midst of these campaigns, Louis by a stroke of diplomacy had suddenly obtained promises of a large share in the coveted Spanish possessions; but it was a deep secret; a trump card, to be brought out when the sickly Spanish king had changed his living death for an official decease. Its weak point was that Leopold had been induced to accept partition from a belief that he would have no heirs; as soon as this belief was dispelled, he naturally insisted on the rights which he derived from his wife and mother. But meanwhile Louis could well afford to be both generous and demonstrative; he was demonstrative when he followed Condé to the capture of Franche Comté in February 1668; and he was generous when, on returning from this campaign, he accepted the proffered mediation of English and Dutch envoys, tendered in accordance with the terms of the Triple Alliance. The result was a treaty—that of Aix-la-Chapelle (April 1668)—whereby Louis acquired Charleroi, Douai, Tournai, Courtrai, Armentières, and Lille, and surrendered Franche Comté. Substantial gains were thus coupled with an important concession; but the secret treaty of January 1668 was Louis's private consolation for the surrender; and moreover he claimed that, by this show of moderation, his reputation was enhanced. Thus quickly was he deflected from the policy of seizing the whole of the Spanish Netherlands by force of arms. A spectacular campaign, a secret treaty, and a public demonstration of morality—these were the profuse substitutes for the singleness of purpose generally to be found in more normal statesmanship.

A patient monarch might have been content to consolidate these conquests, and wait until the fruits of the secret partition could be reaped, especially as every prognostication favoured the early death of the Spanish king. But Louis was one for whom even temporary inactivity was the worst of sins. He had cause of complaint against two of his neighbours—the Duke of Lorraine and the Dutch. The duke was not proving a faithful vassal of France; so in 1670 a French army expelled him from his capital (Nancy), and Lorraine became temporarily French. As regards the Dutch, a number of conflicting considerations appear to have influenced the French king; and it is necessary to distinguish these.

There was first the economic consideration. England had already waged two wars against the Dutch in order to contest their control of the world's carrying trade, and their enforcement of monopolies in the East Indies and in West Africa. France was almost equally concerned; because French products were an important element in the scheme of things whereby the Hollanders waxed rich; for the Dutch ships carried herring to French ports and took away wine and brandy which they exchanged for naval stores in the Baltic and German ports; a trade of short journeys and quick returns; of benefit to France, it is true; but more obviously to the advantage of a commercial rival. Trade with the French colonies was another asset in Dutch commercial supremacy. Modern economists would argue that the English and French were indirectly benefiting from Dutch enterprise; but seventeenth-century statesmen did not look at it in this way. They assumed that Dutch prosperity must be at the expense of rival nations; that it was based on the exploitation of the colonies and natural products of others; that the competition from this source must be met by prohibitive tariffs, or by laws enforcing exclusion, or by war.

Concurrently with the English commercial war on the Dutch there was a French one directed against the same nation. It was conducted by Colbert, who showed determination to wage it, even at the expense of French interests. In 1664, when he founded the East and West India Companies, he placed a moderate tariff on foreign imports into France. As this measure did not achieve all that was expected, he imposed in 1667 a tariff so heavy as to be not fiscal but prohibitive; and the Dutch themselves admitted that its enforcement would destroy a substantial part of their trade. They retaliated in kind; but nevertheless they well knew that their economic polity, which flourished best with free-trade neighbours, would be ruined if competitors succeeded in excluding their ships by prohibitions and customs barriers. Still more so if these competitors combined. In 1669 there were active negotiations for a customs union between England and France, specially directed against the Dutch. Thus, without the expenditure of a single bullet, France could diminish the commercial supremacy on which the strength of the Dutch was based; in conjunction with England she could destroy that supremacy.

Thus far, French policy was perfectly consistent with the current principles of political economy; and the Hollanders paid it a tribute by the fears which they expressed. But at this point the judgement of both Louis and Colbert became confused. The latter, not content with the steady results of his economic pressure, now advocated a war of annihilation against the United Provinces, because thereby he would be able to take over their shipping and industries. Aberrations even more serious now deflected the vision of Louis. He was not interested in economic matters, which he wisely left to Colbert; but he had a very high moral sense. His correspondence at this time is full of righteous indignation—the Dutch, by joining the Triple Alliance, had betrayed him; in return for the 'sacrifices' he had made on their behalf they had joined their old enemy England against him; to make matters worse, they were insulting him in lampoons and caricatures. All the evidence shows that Louis was genuinely moved. As the exponent of good faith and the instrument of the Almighty he would punish this upstart race by first occupying their territory and then imposing his own conditions. These words are little more than a translation of his own.

Nor was this all. Charles of England had also betrayed him; but his bad faith seemed a different thing altogether; something which might almost be expected and understood in a Stuart; moreover it was known that Charles was obliged to some extent to shape his policy in accordance with English opinion. Still more, Charles was a likely convert to Catholicism and a suitable sub-king in a French world. In 1669 came the announcement that the Duke of York had declared his Catholicism; and that his brother, though keenly sympathetic, could not yet follow suit because of his subjects. It was an occasion which called out all the idealist elements in Louis's character. He would now couple retribution on the wicked with promotion of Catholicism in a country where the faith had once ruled. He would subsidize Charles to join with him against the Dutch, and the two would then share the spoils. With an army and fleet in being, and a successful war to his credit, his ally would then be able to 're-convert' England by the methods of which Louis himself was afterwards to give an illustration on the revocation of the Edict of Nantes. Here at last was a project worthy of a great king; for it combined three magnificent things—religion, glory, and revenge.

As these three things came into the foreground the economic motive faded into the background; the question of frontiers had scarcely been considered; and even the Spanish Succession was, for the moment, completely forgotten. Since the negotiations for the commercial treaty between England and France were not making much headway, it was agreed to continue them merely as a cover for the more important secret treaty between the two monarchs. In consequence the commercial treaty was never completed; its place was taken by the Secret Treaty of Dover (May 1670) by which Charles, in return for subsidies, undertook to supply a certain number of ships and men for the war against the Dutch; but he was left free to choose his time for announcing his conversion. He had (according to his correspondence) become so religious that he wished to make the declaration at once; but Louis restrained him, as the successful war must come first; after which the enforcement of the change on England would be more certain of success. To make assurance doubly sure, Louis employed his diplomatic machinery to effect the isolation of Holland. Having completed these almost superhuman preparations, he dispensed with the formality of declaring war; and in June 1672 two French armies, having a total strength of 120,000 men, were poured into Dutch territory.

The invasion was quickly followed by a revolution. Overwhelmed by the weight and suddenness of the attack the States-General at first sued for peace; but so humiliating were Louis's terms that they were rejected, and the Dutch determined to fight for their existence. John De Witt rallied all the forces of the United Provinces, and might well have proved himself as great in this as he had proved in earlier crises; but the pro-Orange and anti-burgher party was strong as well as vindictive. De Witt and his brother were murdered at

The Hague by a mob in July 1672. Supreme command was then entrusted to the young Prince William of Orange, who was already maintaining a strong defence against the invaders. He was assisted by nature; for there were heavy rains in the autumn of 1672, and Amsterdam was saved by opening the dykes; soon the magnificent French armies were marooned in the floods. Nor did Louis and his English ally fare much better at sea. Several indecisive naval actions were fought, including the Battle of Texel (1673), but the French commander D'Estrées did not co-operate whole-heartedly with Prince Rupert; nor did the French navy perform all that was expected of it. In consequence troops could not be landed on the coast; and early in 1673 Louis deemed it expedient to withdraw his army of invasion. The occupation of Dutch territory had been marked by several atrocities, including the burning and hanging of peasants and burghers; these were due not so much to the licence of the French soldiery, as to the systematic policy of Louvois, who was steadily displacing Colbert in the counsels of Louis.

Soon the French king was deserted by his recently-purchased allies. The Emperor, Brandenburg, Denmark, and Brunswick all forsook his cause; even Charles, still an undeclared Catholic, was obliged to make peace with the Dutch early in 1674. Worse still, the Dutch obtained confederates in the Emperor, Spain, and the Duke of Lorraine, and these were united in alliances directed against France. Only Sweden remained faithful to Louis.

Thus within two years of launching the Grand Design, its ignominious failure had been demonstrated; neither revenge nor glory had been achieved, and the prospects of Catholic propaganda in England seemed as remote as ever. Other rulers might have seen in the collapse of such schemes the punishment entailed by arrogance and cleverness; but Louis was not fashioned as ordinary men. He had enormous reserves of manhood, money, and talent at his disposal; the diplomatic machinery controlled from Versailles was the most elaborate ever known; and above all he had a supreme sense of the justice and morality of his cause. Without a moment's delay the Dutch affair was side-tracked, and the road was cleared for more customary freights. If he could not take The Hague or Amsterdam, he would take Brussels or Antwerp; out of failure he would create success.

In this way, therefore, the punitive expedition of 1672 became a general war by 1674. For the second occasion Franche Comté was invaded and at the same time Turenne completed a general devastation of the Palatinate. In this way, a new turn was given to warfare; for whereas hitherto such ravages had been the work of undisciplined soldiers; here was a concerted devastation of a peaceful province by soldiers acting under orders. These orders came from Louis and Louvois. In a series of brilliant victories Turenne then expelled the German troops which had invaded Alsace; it was in one of these battles that he was killed (July 1675). Another loss was that of Condé, who retired from service in the same year, a year notable also as that of the Battle of Fehrbellin, when France's only ally, Sweden, was defeated by the Elector of Brandenburg. By 1676 the war was being most fiercely contested in Flanders and in the Mediterranean. Admiral Duquesne defeated the Spanish and Dutch fleets off Sicily; but De Ruyter was mortally wounded in action (April 1676), and Messina was then occupied by the French. In Flanders there were numerous sieges, at which Louis himself took part; these were resumed in 1677 when Valenciennes and Courtrai were captured, and the Prince of Orange was defeated at Cassel. In the Rhineland, the French troops took Freiburg.

But in spite of these successes Louis was now anxious for peace; because the war was making heavy demands on national resources, and his successes were not commensurate with the expenditure in men and money. It was characteristic that while his generals went on winning battles, Louis was straining every diplomatic device in order to end the war; that he had such difficulty in doing so serves to prove how, even in the motley array of enemies ranged against him, some degree of unity had been created by hatred of France. Hence the French policy of breaking down this temporary unity by fomenting jealousies and quarrels in the allied ranks. Thus, the Dutch burgesses were mostly anxious for peace and a restoration of commercial relations with France; they were accordingly bribed by a promise of the more lenient tariff of 1664 in place of that of 1667. William of Orange was as resolutely opposed to peace (in spite of his many defeats); so it was not difficult to set him against his compatriots. In England, Charles was being paid to retain his neutrality; but his Parliament was urging him to declare war on France; so Louis subsidized Parliament also; thus using one fund to retain Charles in the French interest, and another fund to induce the Commons to keep him in that interest by refusing him supplies. Bribery was also employed to effect the same sterilizing process in Germany; never indeed was French diplomacy more active, nor French money in wider circulation. For what purpose? To induce his opponents to end a war in which he alone was winning battles. This proved that Louis had brought into existence something new in European politics; a certain solidarity, precarious and suspicious of itself, but acquiring some cohesion and even spirit when opposed to a military power which threatened both the independence of every small state, and the integrity of every international obligation. It was partly because of this, and partly because he loved sieges that Louis, so far from pressing through to Brussels or Antwerp succeeded only in capturing towns near the frontier.

In proportion to his military successes his demands were very moderate; indeed he was not even claiming all the conquests he had made. There was a rich variety in the methods he adopted to secure a settlement. Early in 1678 he abandoned Messina as a proof of conciliation; a few weeks later he captured Ghent as a proof of power; everywhere his agents were pouring out money like water in order to detach this opponent, or to set others by the ears; throughout it all he was using every resource afforded by wealth and cleverness to end a quarrel of his own making. He wanted restitution of her lost territories to his Swedish ally; for himself, Franche Comté and several Flemish towns, including Valenciennes, Cambrai, Condé, Aire, and St. Omer, all of which were already in his possession. Franche Comté he had surrendered in 1668; now he held it for the second time; Valenciennes, Condé, and Cambrai were necessary as outposts for the protection of Artois. The true test of Louis's diplomacy lies not in the skill with which he sowed dissension among his enemies, but in the comparison of his objects in 1678 with those of 1672, and still more in the contrast between the ease with which he resorted to arms and the difficulty he experienced in obtaining peace.

For some time negotiations had been proceeding at Nimeguen, and the French king at last secured peace by detaching the Dutch from their prince, and consenting to the abandonment of his claim on behalf of Sweden. On the last day of July 1678, a treaty was signed with the States-General, whereby Louis restored Maestricht and the tariff of 1664; this was followed by a settlement with Spain, also signed at Nimeguen. By this, France restored most of the Flemish towns she had acquired by the Treaty of Aix-la-Chapelle; she also surrendered more recent conquests, such as Limburg and Ghent; in exchange, she acquired Franche Comté, Cambrai, Condé, Cassel, St. Omer, Ypres, Valenciennes, and Maubeuge. These were important gains; but they were counterbalanced by the fact that of the abandoned conquests, Charleroi, Binche, Ath, Courtrai, and Oudenarde were now erected into a substantial barrier against further French aggressions in Flanders. In effect, therefore, while Franche Comté was a great acquisition for the middle-east frontier, the all-important north-eastern frontier was as weak and indeterminate as before. By the third treaty, that with the Emperor (January 1679), France received Freiburg in return for Philippsburg, and restored the Duke of Lorraine to his duchy, with the exception of Nancy and Longwy. Finally, in June 1679, Frederick William was induced to restore to Sweden his conquests in Pomerania, and in October, by the Treaty of Saint-Germain-en-Laye, the elector promised to vote for Louis at the next imperial election, and to induce his brother electors to do likewise; the expressed motive for this promise being his admiration for the heroic qualities of Louis. So at least one enemy of France was quickly won over again.

Before these treaties were signed there had occurred an event which was ultimately to bring more closely together the two Protestant nations who believed that the success of Louis meant glory for himself and slavery for everyone else. This was the marriage of the Prince of Orange with Mary, daughter of the Duke of York. The alliance was destined to provide a strange commentary on the Secret Treaty of Dover. Meanwhile, there was a feeling in France that the Peace of Nimeguen was a very unsatisfactory conclusion to a war which had cost so much in men and money; and there now entered into men's minds a doubt whether guns and diplomats were the sole requisites for national progress and pre-eminence. Even more, there was this certainty that there could be neither peace nor security in Europe so long as Louis was King of France.

5
Louis the Ruler of France

LOUIS CAUSED A record to be drawn up of the main principles which inspired his policy. The *Historical Memoirs*, written specially for the guidance of his son, the Dauphin, were compiled by editors under his supervision, probably in the years 1666–9; for this reason they take rank in the literature wherein kings expound the mysteries of their craft. It is true that the editors do not indulge in those flights of humour or irony which make Frederick the Great so readable; nor did they command that erudition, sacred and profane, which give such weight to the statements of James I of England; but nevertheless, the *Memoirs* authorized by Louis are remarkable for frankness and clarity, and they throw some light on his general principles of government.

God is defined as 'a superior power, of which our royal power is a part'. Kings are 'absolute sovereigns, having full disposition of the goods of their subjects, both lay and clerical'. Kingship is described as an exacting profession, perhaps the most strenuous of all careers; because it requires continual application to business, personal study of the minutest details, and a power of subordinating one's feelings to the interests of the State. For example, a king may have his love affairs, but these must be kept in their place; they must not interfere with the daily routine; the harem and the cabinet must be kept quite distinct. The true king combines two things—a man, subject to passion and error; and a living embodiment of the State, a bloodless personality which, like a corporation, knows nothing of sin or regret, and must function every day with the same inevitable regularity. Hence, a transcendental morality and intelligence distinct from those of the ordinary individual. One instance of this transcendental morality is provided; how he kept his word with the Dutch when he went to their aid in 1666, and how Spain was so touched with this evidence of good faith that her Government entrusted him with the personal safety of Margaret, his wife's half-sister, when she went from Madrid to Vienna in order to marry the Emperor Leopold. It is not a very clear illustration of either moral conduct or its reward; but it was the example chosen by Louis. Another virtue he couples with good faith—moderation. In illustration of this he cites the concessions which he made at the Treaty of Aix-la-Chapelle, and how these helped to establish confidence among neighbouring states. Here again, he informs the Dauphin, he had his reward; for the Emperor thereupon signed the secret treaty of partition with him. This illustration is weakened by the fact that the partition was made before and not after the Treaty of Aix-la-Chapelle; but the moral lesson is the same nevertheless. Louis would not, however, push scruple to extremes. There are occasions when, in the interests of the State, the king must violate his faith. This is specially true of treaties, which are full of compliments and assurances of eternal friendship; but nobody takes these seriously; for they are merely diplomatic embroidery; and hence there may justifiably be secret infractions of such obligations; indeed 'everyone expects that there should'. These are among the most noteworthy of the principles formulated by Louis XIV for the guidance of his son.

'Holding as it were the place of God we seem to participate in his knowledge.' This is the keynote of Louis's policy. Inspiring his industry and application was this implicit faith in the divine intention of his kingship. It was not an unusual nor, at that time, an unreasonable claim; for its appeal was directed to the instinct for worship innate in man, and it attributed the origin of sovereignty to a source less artificial than the social contract; the exceptional thing was that Louis acted on this principle with a consistency and conviction without parallel in history. It is because of this sense of high purpose that he has so often been contrasted with idle or dissolute kings, and assigned such exalted place in the annals of monarchy.

Louis's rule may be considered briefly according as it concerned the Court, the Church, and the Nation.

Ever mindful of the Fronde, Louis completed the atrophy of the

French nobility. This he did at the great palace of Versailles, the most enduring monument of the reign. Here, on sandy wastes he constructed architectural triumphs which, better than anything else, attest the monarch's love for spaciousness and lavishness. Though commenced in 1669, the palace was not finally completed until 1710, and throughout these years thousands of men were actively engaged in excavations and building. A chapel in marble and porphyry; avenues and parks decorated with fountains and statues; orangeries, woods, and immense vistas; all these took shape under the direction of a king who loved to superintend every detail of this magnificent memorial. Not the least magnificent thing at Versailles was the King himself; there alone was his natural setting, its quiet greys and greens providing the best background for the flaming scarlet of the King's shoes and the tossing ostrich plumes of his hat. Bright flowers and tuneful sounds were among the few things that he loved passionately; nor did he spare any effort to procure an abundance of both; for even when conducting a campaign his thoughts were always of his palace and its gardens; and when he could not have his carnations or tulips he had his violins and hautboys. In the royal chapel mass was sung by a choir of select voices; dinner was taken to the accompaniment of the twenty-five violins known as the Grand Band, and another cohort of skilled instrumentalists officiated at fêtes and hunts. Music was an essential part of the routine of the Court. The Italian Lulli, supervisor of the King's music, made opera so popular in France that even the nobility were allowed to take part in it without incurring social stigma; most of the librettos were supplied by Quinault; and except for the absence of humour and the more recondite harmonies, the partnership of these two had the national importance which attached to that of Gilbert with Sullivan. The florid genius of Lulli accorded well with the monarch's taste; and in *Roland*, one of the best-known of these operas, was depicted the triumph of glory over every other passion, including even love.

At Versailles, in surroundings of almost barbaric splendour, were the Whitehall and the Monte Carlo of France. Here Louis read the despatches of his ambassadors, or penned his diplomatic memoranda, or received the envoys of foreign states; here also the nobility paid obsequious service of an oriental exactitude to a new Jehovah who functioned with such invariable regularity that it was possible to tell the time by observing his acts; or they exchanged fortunes at the card tables, which came out with the candles. At Versailles men lost their money and women their honour, but always in artistic surroundings; for there were canvases of heroic proportion in the Grand Gallery; there were frequent performances of the comedies of Molière or the tragedies of Racine; and if one were insensitive to these things, there were yet the furniture and the tapestry to compel admiration. There was a profusion of gilt and colour; of contrast between the small noisome apartments in which the courtiers slept and the great public chambers in which the King held state; but it was exotic, and was no place for the natural frankness and wit of the French people. It remained the residence of the French monarchy until 1789; in 1830 Louis Philippe made it a national museum.

The Queen took little part in this public life. Her place was at first taken by Mademoiselle de la Vallière, one of the maids of honour to the Duchess of Orléans, by whom Louis had two children; in 1667 she was succeeded by another maid-of-honour, Madame de Montespan; of whose children three survived. These five natural children were all legitimized, and so were given a contingent right of succession to the French throne. In 1684, one year after the death of Maria Theresa, Louis married the nurse of one of these children —Madame de Maintenon, widow of the poet Scarron; but the bride was not accorded the status of Queen. She was in a class quite different from that of the women in whom Louis had hitherto taken pleasure; for she had refinement and a sympathetic understanding, and she influenced her royal consort by her qualities of mind and character. It is difficult to prove that she exercised a restraining influence on Louis; indeed it is more likely that she deepened and hardened her husband's piety, and created in him a greater solicitude for his spiritual welfare, soon to be reflected in his attitude to heretics; but of Madame de Maintenon's charm there can be no doubt; and in these lines which Ahasuerus addresses to Esther, it is certain that Racine depicted the royal consort:

Je ne trouve qu'en vous je ne sais quelle grâce
Qui me charme toujours et jamais ne me lasse.
De l'aimable vertu doux et puissant attraits!
Tout respire en Esther l'innocence et la paix;
Du chagrin le plus noir elle écarte les ombres
Et fait des jours sereins de mes jours les plus sombres.

Of the other personages in the royal entourage there was the
Dauphin, born in 1661, Louis's only son by Maria Theresa. His
education was conducted by Bossuet, and special editions of the
classics were produced for his use: he died in 1711, after an un-
obtrusive life. Another personage who was completely over-
shadowed by the monarch was Louis's younger brother, the Duke of
Orléans, who, on his death in 1701, was succeeded by his son, afterwards famous as Regent. The youngest generation was represented
by the three sons of the Dauphin, namely, the Dukes of Burgundy,
Anjou, and Berry; of whom the first died in 1712, leaving an infant
son, who was afterwards king as Louis XV, while the second became
King of Spain by the will of Charles II. The Duke of Berry died in
1714. Thus narrowly was the succession maintained in the legitimate
Bourbon line. Louis admitted neither his son nor brother to his state
councils.

Versailles helped to bestow on France an eminence in the arts of
peace such as she already possessed in the arts of war. It was in this
respect that Louis's rule had most beneficent results. However
much his policy may have injured France and Europe, he made
Versailles the symbol of his race; of a France universal and omni-
potent; typified not by the strutting cock, but by the flaming sun;
always tempered nevertheless by the embellishments and refine-
ments of an artistically-minded race. The numerous imitations were
tributes to the pre-eminence of his Court. All this helped to
strengthen national consciousness, and to create for it a rallying point;
more, indeed, than any other king Louis had this flair for publicity
and propaganda, and round him revolved a whole planetary system,
every world illuminated and energized by the sun at the centre. It
was sometimes difficult to determine whether this portion of the
universe was inspired by an intelligent purpose; had Louis himself
been asked, he would probably have answered that its motive was
Glory, a personal transcendence, which raised the whole nation on
its wing. But his successors had neither the assiduity nor the money
for a successful maintenance of this tradition.

This unified nationalism is reflected in Louis's policy towards the
Church and the Huguenots. In regard to the first, it should be
recalled that in several Catholic countries, notably in France and
Spain, there had already been effected a change not unlike that
which Henry VIII had instituted in England, whereby the Catholic

faith was retained, but the opportunities for papal intervention or influence were carefully limited. Opposed to this ideal of national autonomy in religious matters was that which aimed at the restoration of papal authority, and the subjection thereto of all the Catholic states. To the first has been given generally the name Gallicanism; to the second Ultramontanism. Most of the French clergy were Gallicans; the Jesuits were Ultramontanes; for as representatives of a great international order, they were not concerned in the promotion of secular patriotism; and were sometimes regarded by Catholics as enemies of national independence. In a sense, therefore, the contest was between two sets of spiritual agents—on the one hand the bishops, responsible only to the King; on the other hand, the international religious orders, responsible only to the Pope.

This distinction was accentuated by an incident which otherwise would not have been important. The word *régale* was used in France of those prerogatives that might be exercised by the King in regard to vacant bishoprics; they were of two kinds—the temporal right to apply the revenues to the needs of the diocese during the vacancy, and the spiritual right to make appointment to benefices within the gift of the diocese which otherwise would have been made by the bishop. An edict of 1673 asserted these privileges on behalf of the Crown, except in those cases where exemption had been obtained. Two bishops in Languedoc resisted the decree; Pope Innocent XI declared in their favour, and the death of one of them provided an opportunity for a contest of principle. Had Louis the right to institute persons to vacant benefices in the diocese of the deceased bishop? Or did this prerogative lapse to the Pope?

Louis had already had several disputes with the Papacy, in all of which he had more than held his own; moreover, he had a convenient threat at hand—the annexation of Avignon. As the dispute over the *régale* raised the whole question of the King's supremacy in his own country, it was specially referred to a general assembly of the French clergy which met in 1682. At this meeting the leading spirit was Bossuet, Bishop of Meaux, the preceptor of the Dauphin, a zealous defender of Gallican doctrines. It was he who drew up the Four Gallican Articles which were ratified by the Assembly and registered in the Parlement of Paris; they are therefore an authoritative statement of the relations between the Holy See and the France of Louis XIV. The first asserted the general axiom that kings are not subject to ecclesiastical jurisdiction in temporal matters; the second recognized papal supremacy in doctrine, but implied that even this might be overridden by a general council; the third interposed the canons of the Church and the Gallican rules and customs between the Papacy and France; and the fourth asserted that, while the Pope had the leading part in deciding questions of doctrine, yet his judgement was not infallible, unless supported by the approval of the Church. The Pope did not hesitate to accept the challenge implied by these assertions; and for some time there was a deadlock, during which the Vatican refused bulls of institution to those clerics who had taken part in the Assembly of 1682 and had subsequently been nominated to bishoprics; while, on his side, Louis did not ask for bulls on behalf of those who obtained promotion and had *not* taken part in the Assembly. Eventually, in 1691 a characteristic compromise was reached. Increasing years and the influence of Madame de Maintenon may have modified the attitude of truculence which hitherto had distinguished his attitude to the Papacy; so the Assembly of the French clergy was induced to write a letter cancelling anything that might be inconsistent with papal prerogatives. Thus, the Holy See was mollified; but there still remained the Four Gallican Articles, solemnly registered by the Parlement and ready at any moment to be revived from their state of suspended animation. There was to be occasion for this in a few years.

Increasing zeal for orthodoxy was reflected in Louis's attitude to the Huguenots, as the French Protestants were named. These had at first been an independent community, a state within the state; their political and religious independence guaranteed by the Edict of Nantes (1598), the avowed object of which was to win them over by clemency and the example of their orthodox brethren. After the siege of La Rochelle, Richelieu was obliged to destroy their political separatism; but by the Peace of Alais (1629) their religious independence was preserved; it is important therefore that by Louis XIV's reign the Huguenots had ceased to be a political danger; on the contrary, they were specially distinguished by two things— loyalty and industry. They provided good soldiers and officials; many of them were capitalist employers or rich merchants; they were among the most contented and enterprising of French society. It is true that they still adhered to their religion; and although the

Edict of Nantes remained the guarantee of that religion, the government was still awaiting the fruits of the clemency which had inspired that Edict. Now, nothing is easier than to stultify a law by a mean or niggling interpretation of its clauses. Louis XIV was naturally unwilling to violate a fundamental law; but he had no difficulty in securing such a rigid enforcement of everything not explicitly authorized by the Edict as to make it valueless. He may have been encouraged to adopt this attitude by the belief that many Huguenots had in fact gone back to the old faith, and that only the wicked and recalcitrant remained to be coerced; and it is certain that, among the French bishops and clergy, he found ardent supporters of his ideal, that of a France absolutely uniform in religion; an ideal common in the preceding century, but now becoming somewhat out of date.

So, with increasing pressure the position of the Huguenots was made more and more untenable. After 1666 their lives were subjected to strict inquisition; they were deprived of offices; many of their chapels were pulled down; their children were 'converted' before their parents' eyes; and for the voluntary conversion of adults payments were made from a special fund. A steadily increasing number left the country; petitions to the monarch were tried in vain. In 1684 an inspired Assembly of the French Clergy petitioned that, as the Edict was not being properly observed, it should be withdrawn; this was done in October 1685, by the famous Revocation, which proclaimed that, as the Edict had already served its purpose, it could therefore be dispensed with. It was not the intention of Louis's Government to expel the Huguenots; rather, the object was to retain them in France, and so guarantee their enforced Catholicism; consequently, those who were caught attempting to leave France were sent to the living death of the galleys; while from those who remained was extracted abjuration of their Protestantism by the methods then commonly employed in 'well-conditioned' states—by dragoons. Nevertheless, a large number succeeded in making their escape to England, Holland, Switzerland, and Brandenburg, where their influence was soon experienced, because most of them were highly skilled, and they introduced improved methods of weaving and finishing textiles; they also supplied many men of integrity and ability for State service in their adopted countries. No economic history of these countries can ignore the advantages which they secured by the influx of Huguenots.

The results for France were not so fortunate. Economically, the Revocation meant the ruin of Colbert's enterprises, because the Protestants had played the leading part in these; their faith was also that of many of the foreign workmen and capitalists introduced into France in order to teach new crafts. These men were not expelled, but nevertheless they left the country, taking their capital with them. Louis never realized how disastrous was the Revocation for the industries of his country; and, though his correspondence with ambassadors shows that attempts were made to bring back some of the refugees by force or fraud, he eventually came to the conclusion that they were a good riddance; a view confirmed by Bossuet, who publicly asserted that, by the Revocation, the reign of Jesus Christ was brought within sight. There was still another effect. Among the exiles were many men of talent, some of whom recorded their experiences; these may or may not have been exaggerated, but they served to incite European opinion against Louis, and their published records of atrocities provided an illustration of what the King meant by peaceable conversion to the true faith. The lesson was not lost on England, where James II was gradually feeling his way to the restoration of Catholicism.

Protestantism was not the only variety of religious heterodoxy with which Louis had to deal. From the Catholic point of view the Huguenots were merely heretics, and so their case was simple; but it was not so easy to deal with the Jansenists who, though regarded by many as unorthodox, refused to leave the Church. Their opinions require a word of explanation.

The name is derived from that of a Flemish bishop, Cornelius Jansen, who compiled a long commentary on the theology of St. Augustine and died in 1638; two years later his famous book, the *Augustinus*, was published. Its author intended to do no more than expound the teaching of the Saint; but theology was then full of snares; and though, by his death, Jansen had himself avoided the earthly consequences of falling into these, his book was nevertheless to be the occasion of division and strife. St. Augustine had formulated a theory of Grace according to which this gift, in its full or 'Efficient' form is necessary to salvation; and the gift is always free, in the sense that it cannot be earned. Salvation was thus placed outside the self, and could not be achieved by human merit or effort alone. This view was accepted as orthodox, but the trouble came when it was interpreted. Luther and Calvin had both sought reform through this avenue; and, as an uncompromising intellectual, the latter deduced from Augustinian Grace a doctrine of pre-destination, which became the corner-stone of the Reformed churches: hence the opponents of both Jansenism and Protestantism had to rely on the argument that, while the sources were unim-peachable, the interpretations deduced therefrom were wrong. These interpretations included the view that salvation was dependent not on devotional aids or 'works', but on Divine purpose manifesting itself in a supreme psychological experience; in effect, therefore, eternal bliss was reserved for the pre-ordained Elect; and even to these, only a moderate degree of earthly happiness was apportioned. This was a 'rigorist' application of the doctrine of Efficient Grace; its converse was the laxist doctrine, taught by some Jesuits, which not only brought salvation within reach of all men but allowed a fairly liberal margin for sin and error, a view generally stigmatized as Molinism or Pelagianism; or, more bluntly, Free Will. The extremes of rigorism and laxism were condemned by the Church; but these names were avoided by the combatants themselves, who fought in the arena under the *noms de guerre* of Efficient and Sufficient Grace. Was Efficient Grace too much? Was Sufficient Grace really insufficient? These were the vital problems to be determined in this combat.

Probably nothing more would have been heard of Jansen or the *Augustinus* had not his strict and somewhat gloomy doctrines been preached in France, notably at the Convent of Port Royal in Paris by a Basque named Saint-Cyran, a friend and correspondent of Jansen, who first directed the serious attention of Parisian society to the subject of eternal damnation. The lady superior of Port Royal, Angélique Arnauld, was a member of a *bourgeois* family which had distinguished itself by opposition to the readmission of the Jesuits into France. The Arnaulds had no sympathy with Protestantism or indeed with any heresy; but they were the declared enemies of the Jesuits, and that brought upon them and the *Augustinus* the atten-tions of the Society. Now, at that time, the best means of discrediting an enemy was to prove him a heretic; so the theologians set to work; Jansen's book was minutely examined; and its teachings were com-pressed into five propositions, which were submitted to the censure of the Papacy. In 1653 Pope Innocent X condemned these five propositions as heretical, so the Jesuits scored.

The effect of this condemnation was that all who professed to be guided by the theology of Jansen could now be branded as heretics, in spite of their refusal to leave the body of the Church. To make the matter more complicated, the Jansenists admitted that the five propositions as condemned by the Pope were heretical; but they contended that these propositions were not to be found, in so many words, in Jansen's book. This led to much sparring; for, on the one side the Jesuits argued (rightly) that the propositions accurately summed up the spirit of the *Augustinus*; while their opponents parried this by insisting (rightly) that these propositions were not stated in the book. Hence the difficulty of inducing the Port Royalists to disavow the propositions 'purely and simply' since they generally coupled renunciation with the reservation that the five propositions had never been enunciated by Jansen. Meanwhile, in 1648 a community of nuns from the Paris Port Royal went back to the old building at Port Royal des Champs, in a secluded country spot near Versailles; so there were now two centres of Jansenist influence in France.

These might seem to be matters merely of theological interest; but theology then played a considerable part in public life; and the Jansenists were to prove an important element in French thought and society during the reigns of Louis XIV and his successor. Soon there were two establishments at Port Royal des Champs—the formal society of nuns in the monastery; and, near by, at 'The Grange' an informal community of men who were either professed Jansenists or in sympathy with them. Among the latter was Pascal; and with this adhesion of strength, the movement acquired an intellectual distinction such as neither the Arnauld family nor the two convents could have conferred. Setting aside the theological controversies which served to brand these men and women with a distinctive name, it may be said that the Jansenists were trying to do for the Church something of what had already been achieved by earlier reformers; but only something, because they never admitted that they were a sect. Like all revivalists, they believed in the need for restoration to simpler and more primitive models, such as had been formulated by St. Paul and St. Augustine; in consequence, they would have discarded a great part of medieval and post-medieval accretions, and with it much of the moral theology taught by later theologians, notably the Jesuits. In particular, they believed free will to be an old heresy under a new name; they insisted on the necessity of the sacraments, and also on the need for more strict preparation before partaking of them; in general, they retained the Catholic life, but they made it strict and uncompromising. Some of them considered religion an intellectual rather than a spiritual experience; all of them analysed the emotions, rejecting everything having a sensuous appeal; they made salvation difficult and rare, but overwhelming when achieved. They looked for guidance and reform not to the international orders, but to the native bishops; and they thought of the Church as a national institution, immune from foreign influences, and superior to the Pope.

They were also great educators and moralists. As educators, they anticipated certain elements in modern educational practice; their textbooks were the best obtainable, and long remained standard works; in preference to the exclusive use of Latin, they encouraged proficiency in the vernacular, and they popularized the study of Greek literature. As moralists, they were the strongest bulwark against the atheism and libertinism which, in the middle years of the century, were fashionable in Paris; and they resisted the more alluring Epicureanism, or indifference to religious distinctions, which had been popularized by Montaigne; indeed, they taught, and many of them exemplified a strict standard of integrity at a time when many forces were combining to undermine it. They acquired fame from the support given them by the *Lettres provinciales* of Pascal, a scathing exposure of the lax principles advocated by some Jesuit casuists; the movement also attracted many notable converts, and something of its spirit was reflected in the austere genius of Racine, one of their most famous pupils. Their high seriousness was a guide and inspiration for Pascal, as it was afterwards a subject of ridicule for Voltaire; and both men were intellectually representative of their age.

In 1669 a compromise, known as the Peace of Clement IX, conferred a precarious immunity on the Jansenists; and for some years the Port Royals continued their activities; the most notable of their expositors being first Anthony Arnauld and then Pierre Nicole. The Archbishopric of Paris was conferred in 1695 on Cardinal Noailles, who was known to be in sympathy with the movement; and thus it might well have seemed that peace was assured. But once again the theological arena resounded with the shouts of battle. The Jesuits had already played havoc with Jansen's *Augustinus*; they now turned to a book published in 1678—Quesnel's *Réflexions morales sur le Nouveau Testament*. Quesnel had emphasized some of the distinctive Jansenist doctrines, including the necessity of free access to the Scriptures; the need for observance of the Sabbath; the irresistible power of Grace, and the fruitlessness of human effort; opinions which had passed almost unnoticed in 1678; but twenty years later conditions were different, because the Society had now the support of the King, through his Jesuit confessors; and, as Louis himself coupled his increasing difficulties at home and abroad with a diminution of divine approval, he was naturally anxious to suppress heresy. Accordingly, he was induced to ask Pope Clement XI to condemn the Jansenist doctrines. This was done by a Bull promulgated in 1705; four years later Louis ordered the two female communities of Port Royal to be abolished, and their inmates to be dispersed to other religious orders. So the ancient edifice at Port Royal des Champs was razed to the ground; and, with oriental thoroughness, the remains of eminent Jansenists were exhumed and thrown to the dogs. Again the Jesuits had scored.

This appeared to end the whole matter; but already the whole Jansenist influence had spread far beyond the limits of the Port Royals, and a controversy of national importance was to be precipitated by Louis's insistence on the suppression of heresy. The Bull of 1705 had condemned, not Quesnel's book but the Jansenist attitude of 'respectful silence' on the question whether the five propositions were to be found in the *Augustinus*; for Louis, this was not enough, so in 1711 he asked the Pope to condemn the heterodoxies of Quesnel, in spite of the fact that these had been enunciated more than thirty years before. With this request Clement XI complied in the famous Bull *Unigenitus* (1713), in which he extracted no less than 101 heresies from an apparently innocent and devotional work. A section of the French clergy, led by Noailles, opposed the acceptance of the Bull, because such acceptance implied the surrender of Gallican principles; in this way Jansenism acquired the powerful backing of all the forces ranged on behalf of French eccleaisstical autonomy; in other words, round Noailles were ranged not only all who sympathized with Port Royal, but all who were opposed to the Jesuits, and so the opposition to *Unigenitus* was not merely theological but national. For Louis himself, the difficulty was that this national attitude confirmed the doctrines formulated for him in the Four Gallican Articles; here was a chance of vindicating these doctrines. But though the King was aware of the strength and patriotism of this movement, he had no option but to enforce acceptance of the Bull which he had himself requested. In August 1715, a few days before his death, he therefore accepted the Bull, and provision was made for its enforcement on Noailles and the opposition by a national council.

Zeal for orthodoxy and the influence of the Jesuits thus induced Louis to surrender one of his own principles; but the controversy was by no means ended by his death. The French clergy and laity remained sharply divided regarding *Unigenitus*; and eventually the Parlement of Paris, as representative of the national or anti-ultramontane party, won the last round by the expulsion (1762) of the Jesuits from France. Thirty years earlier, in the midst of a revival of this old quarrel, the Jansenist doctrine that the Church was superior to the Pope had prompted the public suggestion that the Nation was superior to the King; one of the earliest popular expressions of political dissent in the *Ancien Régime*. Still earlier, some of the exiled Huguenot ministers, notably Jurieu, had revived the doctrine of the social contract, thereby reinforcing the principles which were taught in England by Locke, and exemplified in the Revolution settlement of 1689; moreover, the Huguenot axiom of royal responsibility, together with other characteristically English doctrines, was to be carried back to France by such travellers as Montesquieu and Voltaire. So the triumph of orthodoxy was not won cheaply; for the suppression of both Huguenotism and Jansenism had its repercussion on French thought, and the monarchy necessarily sacrificed some popular esteem by its increasing association with the Jesuits. Herein is a link between the theology of the seventeenth century and the politics of the eighteenth.

But these are remote consequences. Meanwhile the rule of Louis, like that of the Stuarts, was based on what was then the strongest of foundations—divine right. This was less a concerted theory of government than a sentiment, and a sentiment may be more potent and more enduring than a syllogism. It was possibly more widely diffused than in England, as it was not confined to Clergy and Court; it was also more intense, amounting to a passion. The reign of Louis XIV served to strengthen it; but as he had no serious illnesses, and as no attempt was made to assassinate him, it is not possible to cite actual proofs of its strength, which would have been most clearly manifested had the life of the King been threatened in either of these ways. But for the reign of his successor it is possible to apply such a test. In 1744 Louis XV was seriously ill at Metz, and the number of masses for his safety recorded and paid for in Notre Dame was about 6,000; thirteen years later, after Damiens's attempt at assassination, the number dropped to 600; in April 1774 during his last illness the number was 3. This is perhaps the most eloquent commentary of the tremendous prestige created for the monarchy by Louis XIV, and the steady decline of that prestige in the reign of his great-grandson. In England, the collapse of divine right was sudden and complete; in France, it gradually faded away in the fierce light of scepticism and disillusionment.

It was characteristic of *Le Grand Siècle* that what was pre-eminently a human and devotional sentiment was reduced to the formalism and challenge of a code. This was done by Bossuet in his *Politique tirée des propres paroles de l'écriture sainte*, wherein he expounded this thesis: that, as the absolute rule of divinely-appointed kings was the normal characteristic of the Israelitish history depicted in the Old Testament, this must be the polity best adapted for the modern Christian state. As a corollary, criticism of the divine-right prerogative was identified with blasphemy. This was a perfectly valid conclusion so long as the literal inspiration of each book of the Bible was indisputable, and provided it was permissible to detach from its context any passage of Holy Writ and urge it as an infallible rule. It was long before either of these axioms was impugned; but the process had already begun, and was being carried far by the researches of the scientists into the forces of nature. As the older, biblical doctrine refused to yield an inch, and as philosophy and science came to discard all the preconceptions which hitherto had been accepted without question, there were brought into antithesis two entirely distinct worlds of thought; the one clinging to tradition and authority, the other determined to sacrifice all that hitherto had been considered fundamental. This antithesis can be detected throughout the course of the eighteenth century; its continued existence helped to increase the artificiality and instability characteristic of the *Ancien Régime*.

The view that Louis's rule was popular with the mass of the

French people receives some confirmation from the character of the revolts; for not one of these was against the monarchy. The most serious, because the hostilities were prolonged, was that of the Protestants in the Cevennes, who, especially in the years 1702–5, maintained a guerilla warfare in the mountains against the dragoons, and proved a match for the troops led by Villars. In spite of numerous executions the Protestant faith survived among the Camisards, as well as in Dauphiné and in many parts of Languedoc; but the French Protestants were monarchists, and there was no scheme of political opposition behind their resistance to the royal troops. The same is true of the risings caused by taxation. Of these, the most noteworthy were that of the territory of Boulogne (1662) against a tax enforced in lieu of the enforced billeting of troops; that of the Landes in 1664 against the imposition of the *gabelle* on a province hitherto exempt; that of Bordeaux (1675) against new taxes on tobacco and stamped paper. These last taxes were the occasion of a serious rising in Brittany in 1675. The offices of the tax-collectors in Rennes were demolished, and there was fighting in the streets between the rebels and the troops of Militia brought in by the Governor; elsewhere in the province the movement assumed the form of a peasants' revolt against the feudal rights still enforced by the seigneurs. For a few days it seemed that nobility and tax-collectors alike might perish in this mutiny of a whole province. But order was restored by royal troops, and those peasants who fell into the hands of the soldiers were either killed outright or reserved for the gibbet or wheel. More numerous were the victims in those households where soldiers were billeted; and thus was extinguished this seventeenth-century Jacquerie.

France's almost complete acquiescence in the rule of Louis was most notably manifested by the absence of national opposition to the King's violations of fundamental law. It was not known what laws were fundamental; but it was generally assumed that religion, property, and the succession carried with them certain sacrosanct rights. In regard to each of these Louis showed that law was exactly coterminous with his will. By the Revocation of the Edict of Nantes he violated one of the most solemn commitments of the French monarchy; in 1692 he threatened the security of property by an edict declaring his superior and universal lordship over all territory in the kingdom, and demanding one year's revenue from landowners;

in 1714 he promulgated a decree which qualified his illegitimate children for the succession, thereby impugning the legitimist element in the divine-right theory itself. Thus Louis was capricious where other men might have experienced scruple.

Nevertheless, there was not complete unanimity in this devotion of France to the principle of irresponsible rule. Fénelon taught his royal pupil the Duke of Burgundy that the king was made for the people, not the people for the king; and La Bruyère hinted vaguely that the responsibilities undertaken by Louis may have been too much for one man:

If it is too great a responsibility to have charge of a family; if it is enough to be accountable for oneself; what must be the crushing weight of a kingdom? Is a king sufficiently rewarded by the pleasure derived from absolute power, or by the genuflections of his courtiers? I think of the devious and dangerous ways which a king is sometimes obliged to follow in order to ensure public safety; I pass over the desperate but necessary expedients which he often employs for a good end; I know that it is his duty to answer to God for the happiness of his people; and I ask myself; would I be King?[1]

This doubt was expressed less directly in the writings of the great engineer and general Vauban, who died in retirement and disgrace; for his *Dime Royale* (1707), in which he advocated a single tax, equitably assessed, caused such offence to the monarch that its circulation was forbidden, and a copy was burned by the common hangman. Like Fénelon and Racine he sacrificed Louis's approval by the expression of independent opinion. In his few leisure moments Vauban committed to paper his observations on the political and economic conditions of France; and his extensive travels, together with his remarkable powers of observation, give a special value to these opinions; indeed, his writings outline a complete scheme of reform which, had it been capable of adoption, might have saved his country from revolution. These opinions cover a remarkable range of subject. Thus he was against the taking of outlying forts, and would have preferred to base the defence of the eastern and north-eastern frontier on the pivots of Strasbourg, Luxembourg, and Mons. He would have reorganized the army on a scheme of modified conscription, in which the unmarried were to be taken in preference to the married, and allowance was made for special cases of hardship. For the colonies in the west he advocated a constructive policy—the monastic foundations to be withdrawn from Canada;

[1] La Bruyère, *Du Souverain*.

the privileged trading companies to be abolished; the English, he contended, ought to be bought out from their parts of St. Kitts, and Canada should be secured against them by an organized scheme of national defence. He emphasized the strategic advantages possessed by the French in North America, and how valuable was their control of the great rivers; but he noted that none of Louis's wars had injured either of the maritime powers, and he prophesied that one day Canada would fall to English or Dutch.

In regard to religious and political questions he showed a similar enlightenment. Like the Englishman, Sir William Petty (1623–87), he believed in the value of statistics, and was the first Frenchman not only to think that there was a science of statistics, but that it was an essential preliminary to efficient government. He was opposed to the Revocation of the Edict of Nantes and the attempts to convert Huguenots; 'force', he wrote, 'will never make a true Catholic'. He deplored also the abuses to which continued warfare gave rise; namely, the intensification of poverty; the dishonest profits of army contractors; the rise to wealth and power of the unscrupulous; the inequality of sacrifice—death, disablement, or starvation for one, and a fortune or a title for another. As with war, so with government. The system on which the French monarchy rested he thought corrupt; and in his *Dime Royale* he used the word 'gangrene' to describe the body politic; to this inherent corruption he attributed the fact that, by the later wars of Louis, one-tenth of the population was reduced to beggary, and one-half of the remainder was scarcely able to subsist. These were daring assertions from a man in the employment of Louis XIV; he was perfectly loyal, but he spoke his mind. He hinted not obscurely that Versailles was directly responsible for the miseries endured by France, and even suggested that the whole administration had come to be controlled in the interests of women and courtiers. Equally daring was his plea for reform of the prisons; long before Beccaria and Howard he directed attention to this, one of the sombre underworlds which underlay the tinsel and finery of the *Ancien Régime*. The King, he thought, should himself visit the prisons once a year in order to see things for himself; only thus would he realize the horrors concealed by their walls.

Such were the main proposals of Vauban. They serve to suggest that the most effective critic of Louis's policy and administration was the man to whom most of the military successes of the reign were due.

6

The Spanish Succession, 1679–1715

HAD HE ESTIMATED his position in 1679, Louis might well have
thought that it had improved since 1661. For example, economies
could be effected in the subsidy paid to Charles of England, because
that monarch was then so occupied by the Popish Plot and the
exclusion campaign, that there was no danger of either him or his
Parliament playing a part in European affairs; also, the Elector of
Brandenburg had renewed the old alliance, and was followed by the
Elector of Cologne. At home, Louis had just been accorded the title
'Great'; his armies and fleets were steadily increasing in size, and
enemies were not yet able to rival their organization or equipment.
The monarch's readiness for further conquests was symbolized by
his emblem—the Sun, and by his motto *Nec Pluribus Impar*; in
Louvois, he had a devoted servant, and soon (1683) by the death of
Colbert he was relieved of the one minister who did not completely
endorse the royal policy. Such were the advantages. But there was
another side. Charles of Spain still lived; the secret treaty of partition with the Emperor was long since forgotten, and the King, now
entering on middle age, had lost some of the buoyancy, but not the
confidence, of youth. There was also disillusionment. Everywhere,
in the history of recent events, he read a record of perfidy and selfish-
ness; men had accepted his money to betray him; he was surrounded by small, selfish potentates, formidable only in a pack, but
easily disposed of when isolated. From this point may be dated a new
element in the psychology of Louis—that of irritation; from being
militant he had become quarrelsome.

For a time actual conflict was avoided; and a policy was adopted
of enforcing rights which appeared to be justified by impartial

research. The claims by 'devolution' had arisen from investigation into legal practice in the Low Countries; historical inquiry was now utilized to justify claims on territories which, at one time or another, had been dependent on the acquisitions recently made by France. In the old feudal order of things there had been many instances of possessions in one state 'depending' on the ruler of another state; but by the seventeenth century a more modern conception of sovereignty had generally been superimposed on this loose internationalism; and no one could seriously support the argument that, when Louis acquired territory, he was entitled to all the possessions which, at some time or another, had acknowledged the suzerainty of the power formerly ruling in that territory. Some contemporaries even hinted that the argument was a piece of casuistry; others thought that it might prove as ominous as the claims by devolution had already proved.

The annexations which ensued were called *réunions*, that is, the restoration of territories which 'by right' ought to have gone with the parent acquisitions; and a show of legality was given to them by the inspired decrees of local Parlements and superior courts. They began in a moderate way on the frontier of Franche Comté, and were soon extended to Lorraine. Most important were those which followed from the French acquisitions in Alsace. Originally, these had been Imperial fiefs; but the Emperors had granted away so many franchises that there was now much confusion throughout the whole province between competing rights and jurisdictions; a state of affairs admirably suited to the investigations of the jurists who worked against the background of large armies. In this way, several Imperial towns became French, notably Colmar, and, most important of all, Strasbourg (September 1681). In the south-east Casale was occupied; and, after some preliminary manœuvring, the fortress of Luxembourg was taken by storm early in 1684. This was not war, but in some respects more irritating than war. Its immediate result was the sacrifice of an ally, Sweden, alienated by the annexation of the small Swedish possession of Zweibrücken. There were more indirect consequences. The Emperor, it is true, was unable to retaliate as he was more than fully occupied with the Turk; but there was a complete revulsion of feeling among the German princes, whose friendship Louis had hitherto secured at such an expensive rate. Equally impolitic were Louis's methods of safeguarding these acquisitions; namely, stricter alliances with Charles of England and Frederick William of Brandenburg, the two rulers who had most conclusively proved that they were not good value for French money. Frederick William appreciated the French connexion because it gave him further opportunity of acquiring Swedish territory; Charles valued it for the subsidy, because it enabled him to demand (and receive) still more money when Louis's conduct threatened to provoke war.

Inevitably, also, this policy led to the creation of another Grand Alliance against France, that of 1682 which included the Emperor, Spain, Holland, and Sweden; its professed object being to keep France to her frontiers as determined by the Treaty of Nimeguen. Again it seemed likely that Europe would be involved in a general war. But an unexpected diversion suddenly altered the complexion of affairs. In July 1683 the Turkish Grand Vizier, Kara Mustafa, appeared before the gates of Vienna with an enormous horde of Oriental and European troops. Before this menace, Leopold fled; and the Pope called on the faithful to embark on a crusade against the infidel. Louis thereupon made the Emperor's position even more untenable by subsidizing revolts in Hungary against him. Vienna and the Empire were saved, not by any of the Western princes, but by John Sobieski, King of Poland, who succeeded in driving the Turks from Vienna.

For a few years, however, this diversion from the East served to stay the hand of Louis in the West. In August 1684 he signed at Ratisbon a truce with the Emperor and Spain for twenty years, in terms of which he retained Strasbourg and Luxembourg. Thus, from the weakness of his enemies he had profited; he had vindicated his right to these important frontier possessions, and he had granted peace as a conqueror. It seemed like a renewal of earlier triumphs, and as if from this point he would advance to conquests even more substantial—the acquisition of Flanders, or even the extension of French territory to the Rhine. It was the climax of his career; not in the sense of achievement, but of expectancy; not because he had defeated his enemies, but because they appeared too weak or divided to oppose his designs. It is from this point, however, that his decline may be traced.

The decline was inevitable when it is considered how insecure were the foundations on which his pre-eminence was based. His agents had served him well only in the policy of immediate advantage. For the Dutch, the peace of 1678 had been a minority peace, and the majority had the leadership of William of Orange; for the Elector of Brandenburg, the French alliance was useful only in so far as it advanced the Hohenzollern policy of territorial expansion; most speculative of all was the support afforded by Charles II of England. By bribing Charles, Louis had prevented Parliament from forcing England into war against France; and it was a signal achievement of French diplomacy (or rather French money) that a great naval power, capable of redressing the European balance one way or another, was reduced to impotence. But this hired neutrality of England would have been worth the money only if Louis had profited by it to consolidate his European position either by defeating an enemy or establishing a secure frontier, *neither of which objects he had achieved*. Nevertheless, events in England appeared to confirm the wisdom of the French king; for the project of excluding the Duke of York had failed; and so on Charles's death England would have a Catholic sovereign, devoted to Louis, and anxious (with French help) to restore Catholicism in England. Thus Louis had diplomatically won over England, the United Provinces, and Brandenburg; but in two of these states were national majorities seething with hatred of France; while in the third was one of the most astute rulers in Europe, determined to throw over Louis as soon as he had served his purpose. An event of domestic politics served still further to harden European opinion. This was the Revocation of the Edict of Nantes (1685). The Huguenots who found refuge abroad had more influence than the whole diplomatic corps of Versailles.

At this point allusion may be made to a minister by whose advice Louis's conduct was to some extent determined. François Michel Le Tellier, Marquis of Louvois, was born in 1641, son of the chancellor Le Tellier, and at an early age he succeeded to a secretaryship vacated by his father. It was by his energy and dynamic force that the manpower of France was made available for active service; in a real sense Louvois created the French army. How efficient were his measures was first demonstrated during the campaign of 1667 in Flanders and that of 1668 in Franche Comté; when the armies which he put into the field had no difficulty in disposing of the hardened veterans arrayed against them. But behind this efficiency was a certain brutal force which had come into greater prominence after

1672; and as Colbert was steadily displaced by Louvois the policy
of the King became more impatient and violent. In some respects
Louvois was the evil genius of Louis. He pandered to the monarch's
vanity and pettiness; he was partly responsible for the two devastations of the Palatinate (1674 and 1689); and he was guilty of special
severities against the Huguenots after the Revocation. Had Louis
been merely a complacent or idle king, it would be possible to
attribute entire responsibility for these crimes to the minister; but
considering the great measure of initiative assumed by the King,
it is impossible to acquit him of a share in these events. Louis
himself, however, appears eventually to have become disgusted with
his servant, and is said to have decided on his disgrace; but this
proved to be unnecessary, as Louvois died suddenly in 1691.
Contemporaries suspected suicide. The tradition left by Louvois
was more permanent than that of Colbert.

Even thus, Louis might well have preserved peace, so overwhelming was the superiority of his arms; on the contrary, however,
he continued to inflame opinion by measures of a somewhat in-
considerate nature. Shortly before the signing of the Truce of
Ratisbon his Mediterranean fleet had bombarded Genoa, because
of the assistance which that republic had given to Spain. After this
successful attack on an open city, Louis required the Doge to go in
person to Versailles in order to beg for pardon, thus coupling disgrace with disaster. The Truce of Ratisbon might well have ended
such enterprises; but in 1685 another small state was the scene of
Louis's activities. This was the Rhenish Palatinate where, on the
death of the Elector (1685), Louis put forward claims to territories
derived from the rights of his sister-in-law, a sister of the deceased
Elector; and just as, nearly twenty years earlier, he had embarked
on a war to assert the claims of his wife, so it now seemed likely
that he would resort to arms on behalf of those derived from his
brother's second wife. Once more, therefore, was the peace of
Europe threatened by the remote consequences of royal marriages.
Almost as provocative was the patronage which the French king
proceeded to exercise over the *bourgeois* peace party in Holland, and
over Victor Amadeus, the young Duke of Savoy. All these measures
were based on the assumption that French predominance was
securely established.

The inevitable result was to be seen in the motley array of powers which ranged itself against France in the year 1686. In the course of that year were formed defensive alliances between the Emperor, Sweden, and Brandenburg on the one hand, and the Emperor and Catholic German states on the other. From these associations originated a league for the defence of Germany, signed in July, the contracting powers being the Emperor, Spain, Sweden, and Bavaria; this was the League of Augsburg. Pacific in purpose, it was unstable in composition; nor did it command any great defensive force. But the Prince of Orange was in sympathy with its objects; and so the peace of Europe was now balanced on such a delicate poise that the least disturbance would precipitate war.

While these associations of leading powers were being formed, Louis was still busy with the small states. For some time he had been vigorously asserting himself against the attempts of Pope Innocent XI to limit the abuse of ambassadorial privilege; soon an event occurred which gave him an opportunity of dictating to the Holy See. This was the affair of the Cologne electorate, a dignity which for long had been little more than an apanage of the Bavarian Wittelsbachs, a house over which Louis had exercised dominance. As the Elector of Cologne was likely to die soon, it was necessary to provide for a successor who would continue the French connexion. With this end in view, Louis chose Cardinal Fürstenburg; by French influence, and against the declared wishes of Pope and Emperor, the Cardinal (by a narrow majority) was elected coadjutor to the Archbishop, and therefore became the strongest candidate for the succession. Attempts were made to annul this election; but Louis signified that he would consider such annulment as a justification of war. Meanwhile, the Archbishop-Elector died (May 1686); whereupon a brother of the Elector of Bavaria was adopted by the Imperial and German interests as the rival of Fürstenburg, and this candidate had the approval of the Pope. At the election, Fürstenburg failed to obtain a clear majority; whereupon the Pope announced his intention of confirming in the Electorate the Bavarian as against the French candidate. Louis regarded this as an affront to his honour, and threatened to annex Avignon; Louvois encouraged him to resort to force, and so troops were sent into Cologne in order to support the claims of Fürstenburg.

It was in this mood of injured dignity that Louis issued his famous *Declaration* of September 1688, in which he contrasted the perfidy and enmity of his neighbours with his own good faith and love of peace; in support of his accusations he cited the League of Augsburg, the denial of his rights in the Palatinate, the opposition to his candidate in Cologne; all these, he claimed, were proofs of hostility to French pacifism. For these reasons he was obliged to resort to arms. Action speedily followed. In October 1688 Avignon was seized; at the same time a large French army invaded the Palatinate and occupied a sector of the left bank of the Rhine. In order to ensure the holding of the Rhenish Palatinate as a base for future operations it was devastated (May and June 1689). Heidelberg, Mannheim, Spire, and Worms were all sacked; the crops were destroyed, and thousands of refugees carried their tales of burnings and atrocities into German lands. This second devastation, however defensible it may have been from a military point of view, was a bad precedent; for in history one wrong always makes at least two.

In the midst of these troubles there had occurred an unforeseen change in the one country where Louis considered his influence supreme; namely, in England. If the calculating director of Versailles could be sure of the wily Charles II, who for the greater part of his reign was dependent on an anti-French Parliament, much more might he hope to control the zealous and devoted James II, whose revenues were sufficient to make him independent of Parliament altogether. The England of Whigs and Exclusion had been succeeded by an England of apparent obsequiousness and incipient Catholicism; and so the Bourbon arrangements for Albion were being fulfilled with the inevitability that follows Divine intentions. French diplomacy knew all about the sects, the republicans, the old Commonwealth soldiery—about everything that might cause a democratic rising; the one thing it had not allowed for was an aristocratic revolution. Of this, there were monitory symptoms as early as James's only Parliament (1685–6), when a nucleus of opposition gathered round Compton, the high-born Bishop of London; and later events showed that James was willing to sacrifice the support of the bishops and landed gentry. An English king who makes such a sacrifice is indeed lost. It is true that Louis saw the danger before James did; and the latter foolishly refused the offer of French help; but the Revolution which followed was a surprise to both; because neither of them realized the tremendous strength of the classes which had been alienated by James's pathetic attempts to copy his paymaster's methods. As the Revolution was both unexpected and bloodless, it provided one more proof that the English were indeed a peculiar people; it was an extraordinary event, for which not even the superhuman machinery of Versailles was prepared.

By the establishment of William and Mary as joint sovereigns in 1689 an entirely different complexion was given to the opposition directed against Louis XIV; for now the Prince of Orange had at his disposal all the resources of a great nation, where hatred of France and Popery was the most pronounced national characteristic. In May 1689, the Emperor and the States-General, by the Treaty of Vienna, entered into an offensive and defensive alliance for restoring European frontiers to the limits imposed by the treaties of Westphalia and the Pyrenees; this was joined by England in December; and so Louis was faced for the first time by a coalition of the two great maritime powers. The alliance was joined by Spain and Saxony; Sweden, Denmark, and Portugal held aloof; the Pope was definitely hostile to France and so the diplomatic isolation of Louis was complete. The war which followed is known, for convenience, as the War of the League of Augsburg. Louis, who had by no means given up his faith in James, continued to subsidize him in his luckless campaign in Ireland, where he was defeated at the Boyne (July 1690); at the same time the French admiral, Tourville, forced the dispersal of a combined English and Dutch fleet off Beachy Head. By the summer of 1690 the war was general; for French armies were then fighting in Flanders, Catalonia, Piedmont, and on the Rhine; there was intermittent warfare between English and French in Canada; at sea there were attacks on merchant fleets, and several projects of invasion were schemed. Against a world of enemies, French resources and organization were strained to their furthest point. In everything but their hatred of Louis the allies were in disagreement; it was in her cohesion and willingness for sacrifice that France was greatest.

The war which lasted from 1690 to 1697 was one of attrition for France. After the death of the Duke of Lorraine there was no one on the allied side capable of effective leadership; and it was only the fervour of William of Orange which kept the coalition together. In 1692, when England had at last cooled in her affection for

William, and there seemed a chance that James might yet be reinstated, a desperate effort was made to redress the balance; for in that year a large expeditionary force was assembled in transports at La Hogue for a landing in England. But the enterprise failed when Tourville was defeated by the allied fleets at the battle of La Hogue (May 1692). In the land operations intended to coincide with this invasion Louis was more successful; for by the skill of Vauban, and the pressure of an army of 50,000 men, he succeeded in capturing Namur. The Prince of Orange attempted to avenge this defeat by engaging the French general, Luxembourg, at Steenkirk (August 1692), but he was again defeated by the superior strategy of his opponent. Luxembourg proposed to invest Brussels; but Louis overruled this, preferring operations against the Dutch, in the hope of wearying them with the war; a characteristic calculation, responsible in part for the continued failure of France to profit fully from the ability of her generals and the valour and organization of her troops. French military superiority was again demonstrated when Luxembourg defeated the Prince of Orange and the allies at Neerwinden (July 1693), capturing 15,000 men and over 70 guns; while at sea, under the command of Tourville the French fleets more than held their own. Thus this war repeated some of the characteristics of that which had preceded the treaty of Nimeguen. French science and organization triumphed wherever they were opposed to allied enemies, who continued to be badly led; but nowhere was any decisive or fruitful victory achieved. There were many sieges, some of them spectacular; and Louis's advantages were continually being frittered away in minor enterprises. His desire for peace increased with his difficulties at home; and by the end of 1693 he was willing, in spite of his successes, to make concessions.

Nevertheless the war dragged on. The allies were as tired of it as was Louis; but no combatant was strong enough to risk a decisive stroke. In 1695 William won back Namur, and English fleets bombarded French ports. As he seemed unable to make any headway, Louis returned to his traditional policy of hastening peace by detaching one of his enemies; accordingly, by the Secret Treaty of Turin (June 1696), Victor Amadeus was induced to come to terms. On his side, the Duke of Savoy undertook to procure the neutrality of Italy, while Louis engaged himself to return Pignerol; thus France surrendered both her ambitions and an outlying fortress in northern Italy. Nor were these all the concessions that Louis was willing to make. He was prepared to recognize William's claim to be King of England, and to disavow the cause of the Stuarts; it was on this understanding that general peace negotiations commenced, with Sweden as mediator. The negotiations were conducted at Ryswick (near The Hague) in the summer of 1697, and the treaties were signed in September and October of that year.

Though the Peace of Ryswick was no decisive settlement Louis was obliged to make some notable surrenders. Among these were Lorraine to its duke; Zweibrücken to Sweden; Freiburg, Breisach, and Philippsburg to the Emperor Luxembourg, with Charleroi, Mons, Ath, and Courtrai, to Spain. French conquests in the Palatinate were restored; the Bavarian candidate was established in Cologne; Pignerol had already been given back to Savoy; the English were restored to their possessions in Hudson's Bay and Newfoundland; and Louis recognized the sovereignty of William. In return for all these, Louis retained Strasbourg. For this change in the fortunes of Louis two things may be held mainly responsible —the combination of the great maritime powers against him, and the increasing exhaustion of France. The first helped to make the war oceanic rather than continental; and emphasized clearly both the importance of maritime communications, and the increasing dependence of the old world in Europe on the new world in the west; the second enforced a certain degree of moderation and even timidity in the conduct of the French king. Even more, at Ryswick, two completely opposed conceptions of sovereignty were for the first time placed in sharp contrast. On the one hand was France, still dominated by the ideals of religious uniformity and military glory, but tentatively reaching out for commerce and colonies; on the other hand were the English and Dutch, Protestant and maritime, under tolerant and constitutional governments, the twin powers which, when united, were powerful enough to thwart the ambitions of the Bourbons.

The settlement really did little more than clear the decks for the major contest now imminent. In 1697 the childless Charles II of Spain was at last really dying, and an heir would have to be found for his vast possessions. Of the numerous claimants two families had a serious, though not an incontestable, title, that of Louis and that of Leopold. The first, a grandson of Philip III, could as husband of Maria Theresa claim on behalf of his only child, the Dauphin, or of one of his three grandsons, the Dukes of Burgundy, Anjou, and Berry; his wife had, it is true, renounced the succession, but on a condition never fulfilled. Leopold, also a grandson of Philip III, derived his claim from Margaret Theresa, younger daughter of Philip IV, and he had in his favour the will of Philip IV which recognized the claims of the Empress, in preference to other claims; but there was some doubt about the descendant on whose behalf these rights devolved. His daughter by Margaret Theresa had married Maximilian Emanuel, the electoral Prince of Bavaria; the issue of this marriage was a son, Joseph Ferdinand, who appeared to have a good claim; but there was a complication, because while Margaret Theresa had never renounced what rights she possessed, her daughter, before marrying the Prince of Bavaria, had been required by Leopold to renounce her inherited rights, as the Emperor wished these to be transmitted to a son. By his third wife, Eleonora of Neubürg, Leopold had two sons, Joseph and Charles; the first of whom was intended for the Empire, the second for the Spanish Succession, while the Bavarian grandson was to be pacified with the Low Countries.

Such was the tangle into which the Bourbon-Hapsburg alliances had worked themselves. There was something to be said for and against each claim. If seniority of daughters counted, then the Dauphin had the better right; for he was the grandson of an eldest daughter and the son of an eldest daughter; if renunciations meant anything, then the Imperial family had the advantage, for neither the Emperor's mother nor his wife had made a renunciation; if public opinion was to be considered, there was this objection to the French candidature that, if successful, the crowns of France and Spain might be united. It was not at first realized that the same objection would apply if Charles, Leopold's candidate, succeeded to the Empire, as he actually did by the death of his brother Joseph in 1711.

Both English and Dutch were vitally concerned in the fate of the succession. They dreaded the prospect of French control over the Spanish colonies and the Low Countries, and they were anxious to avoid another war. As it seemed that something might be obtained by negotiation, their ruler William was induced to come to terms. In October 1698 France, England, and Holland committed them-

selves to a secret partition treaty whereby the infant prince of
Bavaria was to have Spain, the Indies, the Low Countries, and
Sardinia; the Dauphin was to have Sicily and Naples, Finale,
Guipuscoa, and the Tuscan *presidi*,[1] and the Archduke Charles was
to have the Milanese. But Charles II, supported by Spanish opinion,
was against the idea of partition; and so when he heard of this
treaty, he made a will (November 1698) leaving the entire succession
to the young Prince of Bavaria. Within a few months this child died,
much to the relief of his grandfather, the Emperor, and so the
partition projects had to be renewed. In March 1700 by a second
adjustment the share previously assigned to the Bavarian Prince in
the first treaty was transferred to Leopold's younger son, Charles;
otherwise the terms were the same, except that the Dauphin was to
exchange the Milanese for Lorraine. The Emperor repudiated this
treaty. As this partition was equally repugnant to the Spanish Court,
Charles again made a will (September 1700) in which he left the
whole possession to the Duke of Anjou, second son of the Dauphin,
and the younger grandson of Louis. Failing him, the third son, the
Duke of Berry, was to inherit; failing him, the Archduke Charles. In
taking this step, Charles was influenced not by French diplomacy
but by a desire to prevent the dismemberment of his possessions, and
to retain that undivided empire as a bulwark for Catholicism.
Charles of Spain died on 1 November 1700.

After some deliberation Louis decided to accept on behalf of his
grandson the inheritance which Providence had brought to his
family, and the Duke of Anjou was hailed as Philip V of Spain. It
seemed the consummation of the ambitions of a lifetime; and its
immediate effect was the annulment of the recent partition treaties.
The news was variously received in Europe. Leopold and William
at first urged the necessity of war; but neither English nor Dutch
were anxious to engage in hostilities; moreover, William's prestige
in England was very different from that which he had enjoyed in
1689. Other nations were willing to acquiesce in France's acceptance
of the will, and for a time it seemed likely that Philip V might
quietly enjoy possessions far greater than any which his grandfather
had secured by diplomacy or arms. But Louis never knew when to
let well alone. The will had definitely stipulated that the crowns of

[1] These were defended ports on the Tuscan coast and include Orbetello
and Piombino.

France and Spain were not to be united, and acceptance of the will meant acceptance of this condition; yet Louis registered in the Parlement of Paris a solemn declaration safeguarding Philip's contingent claim to the French throne. Thus, scruple for hereditary right was mingled with violation of the testament on which he was acting; once again, the logic of Versailles could be defended only by casuistry or artillery, and European opinion was provoked àt the one moment when it might have been left to slumber.

As if this were not enough, Louis proceeded to fill the barrier towns of Flanders with French troops, and instead of expelling the Dutch garrisons he held them as hostages until the States-General declared their intentions. This was little better than a declaration of war. Even thus, England and Holland were still conciliatory, and William, having gone so far as to recognize Philip as King of Spain, demanded only the evacuation of the Flemish towns. As this was refused, the security of the Dutch was in danger; and their appeal to England met with a chivalrous response; for, by the summer of 1701, even the Tories had come to admit that the menace from France would have to be met by war; and so, before the prorogation in July, 1701, William was assured that Parliament would grant supplies for the pursuit of a vigorous policy on behalf of England and Holland. Meanwhile, Louis still further excited the disquiet of Europe by directing Spanish affairs from Versailles, and governing the Spanish colonies in the interests of French commerce. Of all these challenges there could be only one result—another great coalition against France. In August 1701 was formed the Grand Alliance of The Hague, the contracting parties being the Emperor, England, and Holland. Its avowed intentions were to procure for the Emperor some satisfaction of his claims to the Spanish Succession and, for the maritime powers, securities for their territories and commerce; it was agreed also that captures in the Spanish colonies were to be divided between the two maritime powers, while the Italian possessions were to go to the Emperor. Failing satisfaction from Louis, the allies declared their intention of creating in the Spanish Low Countries a barrier between France and Holland; and they undertook to unite their efforts to prevent the union of the French and Spanish Crowns. Even this was not a declaration of war; but so far from accepting an invitation to compromise, Louis completed his indiscretions by recognizing the young James III as King of England on the death of James II in September 1701. In this way he violated his own promise, given only four years before in the Treaty of Ryswick, and thereby incurred the resentment of the English Parliament, which claimed the right to regulate the succession, in spite of even Louis XIV.

Meanwhile, in March 1702 occurred an event which, on Louis's calculations, ought to have saved the situation in his favour. This was the death of William III. The leader of the coalition was gone; but not before, by his restraint and skill, he had enabled Englishmen of all parties to realize for themselves how serious was the threat from France. Moreover, in the years since 1689 the principles of constitutional government and ministerial responsibility had become established in England; and there was now some degree of connexion between public opinion and the foreign policy of the executive. Equally serious, many Englishmen were now *rentiers*, having invested their money in the National Debt or the Bank of England; and they well knew that the return of the Stuarts would be followed not only by the restoration of Catholicism, but by the repudiation of these debts. Thus, the *rentiers*, whom Louis despised in France, were controlling the destinies of England. This was shown in May 1702, when England, conjointly with Holland, declared war on France. By this time, the maritime powers were leagued not only with the Emperor, but with the Kings of Denmark and Prussia and many of the German princes; moreover, the armies at the disposal of the allies were now as large as those which Louis could put into the field, that is, about a quarter of a million men. But there was one new factor against France, not due to imitation. Hitherto England had been considered a maritime power, never a military power. But now she had the services of a great leader, John Churchill, and of soldiers as valorous as the French. On his side the Emperor had a brilliant general in Prince Eugene, a member of the House of Savoy; while the Dutch had a capable diplomatist and administrator in Heinsius. These three men were the leaders of the opposition to Louis; and together they represented a combination of talent far more formidable than any of which William III had disposed.

In comparison France was not so fortunate. Not only was the country unable to provide the money for another great war, but, even more serious, there was little or no ability in the entourage of

Louis. The places of Colbert and Louvois were filled by men of
inferior stamp, such as Chamillart and Barbezieux, in comparison
with whom the genius of Louis would stand out even more clearly.
This change was reflected even in the generals available for the service
of France. The Duke of Luxembourg (François de Montmorency-
Bouteville), the victor of Steenkirk and Neerwinden, had died
in 1695; Catinat, who had effectively disposed of the Savoyard
military forces in the campaigns of 1690 and 1693, was now in
retirement and disgrace, to be speedily followed by Vauban; and
though among the successors of these men are to be numbered such
able generals as the Duke of Berwick (natural son of James II)
and Villars, mention must also be made of the incompetents, such
as Villeroi, who was partly responsible for the disaster of Ramillies,
and Vendôme who, though he won the battle of Villaviciosa for
Philip V, often sacrificed the cause for which he fought by indolence
and imprudence. For allies, Louis had the Elector of Bavaria, the
Archbishop of Cologne, the Duke of Savoy, and the King of Portugal. Of these the first three were of importance because of the
strategic position of their lands; for a friendly Savoy enabled
France to send troops into northern Italy; while from bases in
Bavaria and on the Rhine Louis hoped both to prevent the junction
of Dutch and Imperialist troops, and to strike at the heart of
Germany. The Portuguese alliance was of service for defence of the
Spanish colonies.

Difference of opinion among his opponents favoured Louis's
cause in the earlier years of the war. There was some siege warfare
in the electorate of Cologne; but in Flanders the allies failed to
effect a landing, and Heinsius did not approve Marlborough's plan
for a general engagement, to be followed, if successful, by the
invasion of France. There was also disagreement between Dutch
and Imperialist over the sovereignty of captured towns in the Low
Countries. In the midst of these disputes the French were profiting
from their base of operations in Bavaria, and in September 1703
Villars defeated the Imperialist and German troops at Höchstädt.
But already France had suffered a serious defection; for in October
of the previous year an allied force captured a great Spanish
treasure fleet in the harbour of Vigo; this decided the King of
Portugal, who by the Methuen Treaty of 1703 resumed the old
alliance with England. The defection of Portugal was followed in

November 1703 by that of the Duke of Savoy, who found that his interests lay not with France but with the Emperor. These events encouraged the allies to adopt a more uncompromising attitude, and accordingly the Archduke Charles was proclaimed King of Spain. It was therefore no longer a war of partition or compromise, but a war of commercial and colonizing countries against the dynastic ambitions of France.

As the issues became more clearly defined, events proceeded more rapidly. France's only ally was now Bavaria. In June 1704 Churchill, commanding a great concentration of allied troops, crossed the Danube at Donauwörth, and entered Bavarian territory, where he joined company with Prince Eugene. A French reinforcement under Tallard came to the Elector's aid and the two armies faced each other on the banks of the Nebel. The Battle of Blenheim (August 1704) resulted in the decisive defeat of the Franco-Bavarian troops; decisive in the sense that it drove the French out of Bavaria and forced Louis to assume the defensive; decisive also in that it dispelled the legend of French invincibility. It was the first occasion on which French military force was faced by armies comparable in size, organization, and leadership with those which Louis and Louvois had built up; it may also have served as an object lesson, since here were foreigners using their enormous resources not for a few spectacular sieges or skirmishes, but for battles of such magnitude as to decide the fate of nations. It must have meant more for Louis than the other events which occurred simultaneously—the surrender of Gibraltar to an English force late in July 1704 and the conquest of Valencia and Murcia by the Archduke Charles.

Inevitably the allies were soon involved in fresh disagreements; this time due to complaints that the Emperor was not giving his full support to the coalition. So Louis was encouraged to make overtures for peace; and again he sought the support of the burgesses of Holland; but he was repulsed by Heinsius; and moreover Marlborough, who coupled diplomatic with military genius, managed to secure a greater measure of unanimity among the allies, in proportion as his influence was consolidated. After this interval, hostilities were renewed early in 1706, and in May of that year Marlborough defeated Villeroi at Ramillies in Flanders, a defeat followed by a far more disastrous retreat and rout. As the battle of Blenheim expelled the French from Germany, so that of Ramillies expelled them from Belgium. This caused Louis to recall Vendôme from Italy, a recall speedily followed by the retreat of the whole French army from Piedmont after its defeat outside the walls of Turin by the joint forces of Victor Amadeus and Prince Eugene. In Spain, the year 1706 was similarly disastrous for the cause of Versailles, and in June the Archduke Charles was proclaimed King in Madrid. Belgium, Italy, and Spain—all these seemed to have slipped from Louis's grasp.

But Providence had not deserted the French king, whose cause was to be assisted in Spain by the one thing which he himself had always ignored—national sentiment. This asserted itself on behalf of the spirited young Philip V, not because he was French, but because he was King of Spain by the will of Charles II. The allies might continue to win pitched battles in Spain, but their troops were not proof against boycott and assassination; and it was a national as distinct from a military movement which restored Philip to his capital. His establishment in Madrid was followed in April 1707 by Berwick's victory at Almanza, when the Franco-Spanish army took 9,000 prisoners; thereafter Spain was practically assured to the Bourbons.

In the year 1707 France experienced determined attacks on all her frontiers; but nothing decisive was achieved, and by 1708 Louis had recovered sufficient strength to resume the offensive. But the enterprise on which he embarked—a naval expedition to the Firth of Forth on behalf of the Pretender—was ill-timed and ill-advised, based as it was on the two assumptions that the recent union with England was unpopular throughout the whole of Scotland, and that the Scots of the east coast had the same religious and political sentiments as the Highlanders of the north-west. In the Low Countries, French troops under Vendôme and the Duke of Burgundy made a surprise attack on Ghent and Bruges; but in July they were defeated by Marlborough and Eugene at the battle of Oudenarde, which, like Ramillies, was followed by a disastrous retreat. The allies then besieged Lille, which capitulated in December. In the Mediterranean the allied forces still held Barcelona, and they succeeded in taking Sardinia, Minorca, and Port Mahon. Thus the resumption of the offensive by Louis had been followed by fresh disaster. Meanwhile France was experiencing the consequences of the war—the shame of invasion; popular criticism of the King's

choice of generals; famine; revolt and misery. It was drab reality
after dreams of glory.

The defeat of Oudenarde, the loss of Lille, and the failure of the
expedition to Scotland all helped to encourage a defeatist attitude
at Versailles; so in 1709 Louis made genuine efforts to secure peace;
indeed, he went so far as to send one of his ministers, Torcy, to
The Hague in order to solicit a settlement. Preliminaries were
accordingly drawn up, Louis agreeing to abandon both Philip and
the Pretender; to guarantee a strong barrier for the Dutch; to
yield Newfoundland to the English; to demolish the fortifications
of Dunkirk; to surrender Strasbourg, and to interpret the Treaty of
Westphalia in the 'German' sense (that is, to restore the greater part
of Alsace). These were enormous concessions and, if accepted, would
have effectually disposed of the French menace; but unfortunately
Louis had himself set a high standard of arrogance when granting
peace to the vanquished, and the allies were following his example
when they added a clause specially intended to be humiliating—
namely, that Louis should lend French assistance for the expulsion
of Philip from Spain. It was on this quite unnecessary clause that the
negotiations broke down. Declaring that he would rather make war
on his enemies than on his relatives, Louis found that for the first
time he had behind him an indignant and determined France. He
pawned his plate, and famine drove men to enlist in his armies in
order to obtain food.

As always, France proved strongest when forced to the wall. On
the north-eastern frontier the incompetent Vendôme was replaced
by Villars who, late in August 1709, took up position with 100,000
men before Malplaquet. Marlborough and Eugene gave battle; the
French fought well and desperately, but their general was wounded,
and their centre was soon pierced by the allied reserves. The retreat
was conducted in good order, and though it was an allied victory,
it had cost such heavy slaughter that it could not be followed up.
In consequence of this weakening on both sides the project of peace
negotiation was again renewed, a project all the more hopeful as
Louis had now abandoned the cause of his grandson; and in a weak
moment he even agreed to pay subsidies to assist the allies to expel
Philip from Spain; but this supreme concession he quickly revoked.
By their harsh demands the allies were injuring their own cause.
With the failure of these negotiations at Gertruidenberg (July 1710)

D

Louis was once more free to assist his grandson; so he sent Vendôme with an army of 25,000 men into the peninsula, and late in 1710 the allied commanders suffered several defeats, notably at Brihuega and Villaviciosa. In this way it was convincingly proved that not all the allied troops could force the Archduke Charles on the Spanish people.

An event of domestic politics was now to exercise a determining influence on the course of the war. This was the substitution in England of a Tory for a Whig ministry (August 1710). Harley succeeded Godolphin; the Duchess Sarah lost the favour of Anne, and so at one stroke Marlborough was deprived of his English backing. Englishmen were tired of the war which, though it had enhanced national prestige, was responsible for increased taxation and complaints of diminished trade; moreover, Godolphin and Marlborough had profited by it to enrich themselves, and opinion was turned against them by the virulent pen of Swift who, in his *Conduct of the Allies*, wrote one of the most scathing political manifestos in English literature. So the Tory ministry was a peace ministry; once more Providence was working for Louis, and in the Preliminaries of London (September 1711) the terms of a general settlement were outlined. Among these preliminaries was the French promise of an Anglo-French commercial treaty offering advantages sufficient to confirm the English ministry in its determination to secure a speedy peace. Another event altered the situation still further in favour of France, namely, the sudden death of the Emperor Joseph in April 1711. As the Archduke Charles succeeded to the Empire, the effect was that a war against Bourbon supremacy was now little better than a war on behalf of Hapsburg supremacy. The stars in their courses were indeed fighting for Louis.

While peace negotiations were being conducted at Utrecht the hostilities continued. Their prolongation was most ardently desired by the Imperialists and Dutch, whose joint army of 130,000 men under Prince Eugene was before Douai in May 1712; against him, Villars could muster only 70,000 men. When the imperialist leader proceeded to besiege Landrecies, Villars decided to risk a battle, since the fall of Landrecies would again lead to the invasion of France; accordingly, he attacked the main body of the enemy troops at Denain on the Scheldt, and forced Dutch and Imperialist to retire in disorder (July 1712). This was not in itself a decisive victory, but it had important moral effects; because the threat of invasion was, for the time, averted, and this was the first serious interruption in the long line of allied successes. Also, it helped to dispose the Dutch to peace; though the Emperor was still irreconcilable. At Utrecht, Great Britain led the way in the formulation of its settlement with France; thereafter the British plenipotentiaries acted as mediators between France and the other powers. The treaties of France with Great Britain, the States-General, Portugal, Savoy, and Prussia were signed at Utrecht in April 1713.

Briefly summarized, their effects were these. In regard to Great Britain, Louis recognized the Hanoverian succession; he dismantled Dunkirk and ceded the Hudson's Bay territory, and Acadia, together with the French portions of Newfoundland and St. Kitts. A commercial treaty imposed the moderate tariffs of 1664 on English imports into France. Philip V was to renounce inviolably all claims to the French throne, and French princes in the line of succession were declared to renounce their claim to the Spanish throne. To the States-General, Louis ceded the Low Countries, with the provision that the Dutch were to hold them as security until they had arranged their barrier treaty with the Emperor. Lille, Aire, and Bethune were restored to France; Luxembourg, Namur, and Charleroi were given to the Elector of Bavaria, pending restorations to his estates. In effect, therefore, the French northeastern frontier was restored to that of 1678. Similar concessions were made elsewhere. Nice was restored to the Duke of Savoy and Sicily was promised to Victor Amadeus. Portugal obtained concessions in South America at the expense of French Guiana, and the Elector of Brandenburg was confirmed in his title of King of Prussia.

By a separate treaty signed in July 1713, Philip of Spain confirmed the English possession of Gibraltar and Minorca and gave Sicily to the Duke of Savoy. This was followed by peace between Philip and both Dutch and Portuguese. Finally, in February 1714, the Treaty of Rastadt established terms between France and the Empire. The effect of this treaty was that while Louis retained Strasbourg and Alsace, he again surrendered Breisach and Freiburg. His allies, the Elector of Bavaria and the Archbishop of Cologne, were restored to their estates, and the Imperial rights in Naples, the Milanese, Sardinia, and Belgium were recognized. These settlements were at last completed by the Barrier Treaty (September

1715), whereby the Dutch were authorized to garrison Furnes, Ypres, Knocke, Menin, Tournai, and Namur, and also to keep the Scheldt closed, in order to prevent Antwerp rivalling Amsterdam. In 1720, by receiving Sicily from Savoy in exchange for Sardinia, the Emperor completely displaced Spanish rule from Italy as he had already displaced it in Belgium; and so these two countries exchanged one foreign master for another.

Such was the settlement which ended the Spanish Succession War.

In that war Louis had experienced misfortune and even disgrace, but at least these had elicited the qualities of fortitude and resignation; moreover, as the embodiment of a suffering and determined France, the old King was not without an element of greatness in these, his declining years. Now that he could look back on more than half a century of diplomacy, expenditure, and bloodshed he might have compared his losses with his gains. Omitting a few small towns and villages, he had added to French territory Dunkirk, Lille, Strasbourg, and Franche Comté. These were substantial achievements, but somewhat modest if the cost is reckoned; for Louis was obliged to consume much of the human and material wealth of his country; his conduct had helped to create a new bitterness and suspicion in the interrelations of civilized states; and, unfortunately for Europe, his great traditions of military glory and international immorality could be emulated by other races, not all of them endowed with a civilization such as that of France. Such were the remoter consequences of the King's lifelong activities. To his subjects he bequeathed a legacy of glamour and bankruptcy.

7

France in 1715

THE RULE OF Louis XIV was absolute, but it was not efficient. A king endowed with his personality and opportunity might have invigorated or moulded the institutions of his country; he might have completed the work of Richelieu, or have swept away the many competing jurisdictions which came between him and his subjects; but none of these things was attempted; and so the monarchy handed on by Louis to his successor was still held together by the clumsy ropework of feudal survival and local immunity. The marvel was that so much energy could still be extracted from the mechanism, and that it held together so long; this may be why Pope Benedict XV claimed that its survival was a proof of the existence of God.

These assertions may be supported by reference to some of the institutions and classes which constituted the framework of the *Ancien Régime*. At its basis was the strong provincialism of France. One illustration of this may be found in the distinction between the Pays d'États and the Pays d'Élections. The latter were provinces such as Champagne and the Bourbonnais which were part of the original apanage of the French kings; geographically, these were mostly central, or at least more central than the frontier provinces, the Pays d'États, which had more recently been added to the monarchy, and still retained traces of local autonomy. In order to distinguish between these different types of province, it should be recalled that the word Election did not relate to voting; for the word had come to mean simply a financial or administrative unit; in general, the Pays d'Élections were more directly under the control of the Crown. On the other hand, in the Pays d'États there intervened between executive and tax-payer representative bodies of three Estates, comprised of clergy, nobility, and burgesses which agreed with the Crown on the total amount of subsidy due from the province, and then repartitioned that amount among the taxpayers. The powers of these local Estates had been weakened but not destroyed by Richelieu; in three provinces, Normandy, Dauphiné, and Guyenne, they had ceased to function altogether; but in 1715 they were still active in Brittany, Artois, Burgundy, Provence, and Languedoc, where they met sometimes annually, sometimes once in three years. The sum voted by these local legislatures was called the Free Gift (*Don Gratuit*), and except for decisions regarding public works in the province, the voting of this sum was the object for which the Estates were summoned.

This association between taxation and representation might well seem to provide an example of constitutionalism in a country which otherwise was subjected to the will of a strong monarch; but in reality it was not so. This may be seen from the relationship of the Estates with the executive. The King summoned these, sending royal commissioners to open the assembly and obtain the grant, and a larger sum than was expected would usually be named by the commissioners; this left room for bargaining, which might be conducted in various ways. One method was to combine the clergy and nobility against the Third Estate of burgesses; not a difficult task, because all three were castes, and the third was despised and hated by the first two. Alternatively, all three could be bribed by the promise of paid offices, or bullied by the threat of their loss; or they might be influenced to some extent by the place to which they were summoned, the executive sometimes choosing for this purpose small towns rather than cities, so that the representatives might not be distracted by outside influences, such as a local Parlement. At the meetings, the Third Estate was placed in a position of obvious inferiority, and was referred to as the *parterre* or pit, where the burgesses sat on benches; while the clergy and nobility had chairs in a front circle; and even if a French Pym or Hampden did succeed in breaking through from the obscurity of the rear, he was sometimes subjected to personal menace; or the town for which he sat might be threatened with the loss of representation. Of all the Pays d'États, Languedoc was that wherein survived the strongest constitutional traditions; but in Louis's reign these were little more than memories;

and in common with the other Estates, those of Languedoc were merely money-voting assemblies. In Brittany, the Estates sometimes made charitable provision for impoverished nobility, and their meetings were the occasion mainly for social entertainment; here is Madame de Sevigné's description of their meeting in 1671:

An infinity of presents; some pensions; a few repairs of roads and bridges; fifteen or twenty tables of hospitality; everlasting gaming; eternal balls; a great show—such are the Estates.

Thus in the Pays d'États some of the forms of representative government were preserved, but none of its spirit. Even more, these local Estates were sometimes impediments to progress. Had these vestiges of separatism been suppressed altogether, it might have been possible to introduce uniform weights and measures, to abolish many local tolls, and even to make the fiscal system more equitable, all of which improvements were seriously considered; but not one succeeded against the tremendous strength of French provincialism. In consequence, therefore, Louis's rule was superimposed on a country wherein there was no uniformity, and where reforms and improvements might easily be thwarted by innumerable survivals from a remote past. France, despite Richelieu, was still semi-feudal.

This may be illustrated from the administration of justice. In the fully-developed state justice is uniform and national, and its administration is an absolute monopoly of the sovereign power. But these are modern axioms. In the France of 1715 men thought of justice not as something abstract and universal, but often as a possessory right, or even as a private perquisite, generally bound up with the possession of land or the grant of an office; for this reason there might be many different kinds of justice, such as that of the King, that of the Church, that of the Seigneur, that of a Parlement. Within these there were subdivisions; for the seigneur might have low, middle, or high justice; he might have his own prison, if he was enterprising enough to maintain it; or his scaffold, if he had 'high' justice; but he could not inflict the death penalty without the consent of the Crown. In addition, there were special courts for mercantile cases between private persons, and for fiscal cases between Government and taxpayer. Even more, just as there was a multitude of jurisdictions, so there was no single jurisprudence valid throughout the whole country; for in the north there ruled the customary law; while in the greater part of the south were the territories of written or Roman law; nor was this merely a geographical distinction; since French legal learning was divided into two distinct and sometimes hostile camps; namely, those devoted to the old feudal or customary rules, and those trained in Roman law who wished to rationalize custom; to reduce it to consistent principles and to embody these in a code. The latter party could utilize, on its behalf, the argument that in the north of France there were recognized nearly 250 different customs, or sets of customary law; with the result that a man owning territory in different provinces would be amenable in respect of that property not only to different courts but to different laws.

In practice, most of the judicial work was shared among public corporations, private franchises, and royal officials. Of the corporations the most important was the Parlement of Paris, in which were combined many of the functions divided in England between Privy Council, Law Court, and Inn of Court; in the provinces there were about a dozen Parlements, including that at Rennes (Brittany); Grenoble (Dauphiné); Rouen (Normandy); Dijon (Burgundy), and Aix (Provence). Only the Paris Parlement had any claim to political influence, mainly because the royal decrees were registered therein; and because it was the scene of the Beds of Justice (*Lits de Justice*) when the King, seated on a couch, made some unusually solemn declaration in the presence of his councillors and magistrates. The numerous presidents, councillors, and magistrates of the Parlements had bought their offices, which were hereditary on payment of the *Paulette*, or tax on the annual revenue derived from such offices. These were the Men of the Long Robe. In addition to civil and criminal justice, all the Parlements exercised some control over police administration, and they had a general jurisdiction over the municipal affairs of the town in which they sat; this naturally led to frequent dispute. Even more, the substantial privileges granted to these close corporations implied in the minds of critics a monopolist and even venal justice; it was often an incompetent justice as well, as some of the magistrates were barely qualified for their duties. Their exclusiveness and intolerance brought upon them the condemnation of the eighteenth-century philosophers.

Another corporation which administered justice was the Church. For this purpose, archbishops and bishops appointed qualified officials who had jurisdiction over matters concerning marriage; questions of church dues; offences against morality, whether committed by clergy or laity; but they had lost their control over wills and probate. Deprivation, excommunication, and penance were the penalties usually enforced. This was quite independent of the justice administered by the many prelates and abbés who, in right of their estates, had feudal jurisdiction over tenants; this might vary in extent from small matters of debt or contract to serious criminal charges not monopolized by the Crown. The lord, clerical or lay, possessing such a franchise employed a trained official, who might commit a guilty person to the seignorial prison (where one was maintained); moreover, the prison, like the private court, might be a source of profit, because of the fees which could be levied. Or it might be a source of amusement, if one had a taste for seeing torture applied to the defenceless; this seems to have been the vogue among some of the smaller nobility of Auvergne, whose brutalities came to light in the grand inquest known as *Les Grands Jours d'Auvergne* (1665–6). Those nobles who were found guilty and had neither money nor influence were hanged. There were also the courts maintained by the municipalities for civil and criminal justice; one municipality might have as many as five such courts. To each of these courts, ecclesiastical, seignorial, and municipal, there was attached a whole army of subordinate officials—the Men of the Short Robe, clearly distinguished by exemptions and privileges from their inferiors the peasants, small tradesmen, and artisans. A Chinaman travelling in seventeenth-century France would have felt at home amid these hierarchies of courts and ranks.

In addition, there was the King's justice administered in local divisions according as they had courts of first, second, or third instance; in these presided trained officials responsible to the King. This was his public justice. There was also his seignorial justice, exercised in military, admiralty, and forest courts; also his feudal justice, in those territories where the land was royal demesne. In forty-two towns of France there was commercial justice, meted out by mayors and corporations with the help of assessors, or specialists in mercantile affairs. Many of the names given to these classifications have been adopted merely for convenience in describing the system; and the above description, by its brevity, implies far more simplification than actually existed. Even thus, it may well seem incomprehensible to those who are accustomed to think of justice as uniform and central. One historical consequence may be mentioned. In England and in the American colonies English common law was regarded with veneration as the guarantee of the liberty of the subject against the prerogative; its principles were already enshrined in such great achievements as Magna Carta and the Petition of Right, habeas corpus, and trial by jury; in France, on the other hand, such an association of ideas was impossible; for there was no national French law; constitutional progress was not directly connected with law, and the administration of justice not merely redressed private or public grievances, but provided the chief 'black coat' employment of the age. Coke and Blackstone were held in highest esteem by both English and American because when these lawyers expounded English law they expounded English rights; but no Frenchman could have thought of Cujas or Domat as other than distinguished jurists, of interest to lawyers alone.

If justice seems complicated, much more was finance. Here again, modern practice makes it difficult to appreciate the problems of the past. Today all the national revenues are merged in one fund, so that deficiency from one source may be wiped out by excesses from another; payments are made from this consolidated fund, not from the separate sources. But in the seventeenth century nations kept these funds in separate compartments, and deficiency in one might cause complete or partial default in the payments saddled on that fund. Hence a speculative element. If a debt or pension was assigned on a tax having a good return, then it might be honoured; otherwise, it might be unpaid. Nor was this all; for it was not uncommon to transfer a payment from a good fund to a less secure one; or *vice versa*; and an enemy or a friend at Court might be the means of effecting such transfers.

More important, the old financiers had no institutions for the provision of credit, nor a civil service for administering revenues; they borrowed money, it is true, but they had to devise means for paying it back. In Louis's reign there was no national bank; tax-collecting was divided between speculators, who took the profits, and unpaid village collectors, who had to take the risk of loss, with imprisonment if they did not make good deficiencies; and, moreover, a large national debt, so far from appearing to be a sign of prosperity, was regarded as a sign of bankruptcy. As there was no bank, money had to be borrowed from private lenders; these might be burgesses, investing in *rentes*, anxious above all for security and redeemability; or they might be large professional lenders, concerned solely for their profit, and generally working in syndicates. As there was no civil service, most of the taxes (but not the *taille*) were farmed out; a block of them might be put up to auction, and sold to the highest bidder; or the auction might be arranged beforehand by someone who, having made his terms privately, was able at the auction to offer a fictitious price. The net result of all this was that only a fraction of the total amount paid in taxes reached the Crown; and in the reign of Louis there was a great increase in the number and the profits of those who came between the taxpayer and the Treasury.

Such a state of affairs might have gone on indefinitely but the matter became much more serious in the seventeenth century when governments were taking more on their shoulders. They were raising bigger armies or navies; engaging in more prolonged wars; or developing colonies; hence a more and more insistent demand for ready money, and (in France) an intensification of the abuses in the methods of providing it. Here is the connexion between Louis's wars of aggression and the deterioration of the internal economy of his country. The Dutch knew the advantage of cheap money and facilities for credit; they had a bank; they had foreign agents equipped with capital, and in their excise they had an equitable means of raising large revenues; England followed their example by introducing first the excise, and later (1694) a national bank. Colbert had tried hard to lead his country in the same direction; but the forces of reaction were too strong, even for him; and he was not accorded the full support of his royal master. Hence France had to content herself with raising money in the ordinary way, by the taxes then in force; or having recourse to what were called the Extraordinary Expedients (*Affaires Extraordinaires*), which were devices such as selling offices, supposed to be reserved for exceptional use. These latter methods became normal and ceased to be exceptional. Meanwhile economists were clamouring for a reform of the standard system of taxation, by which its yield might be vastly improved and its inequalities removed. Louis however preferred not reform of taxation but recourse to the *Affaires Extraordinaires*. It is therefore necessary to consider separately these two distinct methods of raising money in order that the financial difficulties of the Government may be appreciated.

The two characteristics of the normal fiscal administration in 1715 were privilege and inequality. In scarcely two parts of France were the taxpayer's burdens the same; moreover, the unit was not the taxpayer at all, but the person or corporation who could obtain immunity. A noble, an ecclesiastic, a bishopric, or an abbey; these were the individuals and corporations rendering service to the State, in return for which they might plead immunity from most of the taxes; to a lesser extent the lawyer, the official, and the functionary, all these were recognizable units, having some claim to exemption. But it was otherwise with the peasant. He toiled merely to support himself; his superfluity profited only himself; he did not pray for the State and had not at first been forced to fight for it; on him therefore the weight of taxation must fall. Hence the payment of one of the standard taxes—the *taille*—fell most heavily on the peasant; in some of the Pays d'Élections it fell entirely on him. Even more, in many of these provinces its payment was a badge of servitude, and thus a social stigma; and so, for generations the peasant trained himself to evade, as far as possible, this capitulation levy. He hoarded whatever he could save; he lived on the absolute minimum of nourishment, and saw to it that his beasts did the same; he would allow his holding to fall into ruin rather than repair it; he would undertake nothing that involved an outlay of capital. He did these things because he knew that for the slightest evidence of well-being he would be forced to pay an increased *taille*; that if he could not pay the increased assessment, his belongings would be sold for a ridiculous sum; and that if this sum proved insufficient, the floorboards and door of his cabin would be wrenched away in order to supplement the deficiency.

That the personal *taille* actually created impoverishment was the opinion of those who made an impartial study of its incidence. In some parishes it was an instrument for securing vengeance; because one of the collectors might, to satiate a grudge, ruin an enemy by subjecting him to an impossible assessment; equally, the richer members of the village could bribe the collectors in order to obtain exemption. These abuses were mitigated in the Pays d'États, where the levy was smaller in amount and less capricious; in Grenoble, Aix, Montpellier, Toulouse, and Montauban the *taille* fell solely on landed property (*taille réelle*), and was not unjust. The economist, Boisguillebert, was much impressed by the contrast to which this gave rise. In Montauban he discovered a comparatively prosperous peasantry; for there the *taille* bore some relationship to taxable capacity; in Normandy, however, where it was personal and arbitrary, he found not only poverty but depopulation. He instanced a small community of fishermen near Fécamp. These men spent the summer in the Newfoundland fisheries; they represented the kind of population which maritime nations wished to encourage. This community was so hard hit by the *taille* that it disappeared, most of its members going to Holland. Inevitably therefore many of the more prosperous peasants migrated to the towns; or put their sons into the lower ranks of the professions; while those obliged to remain in the fields hoarded their savings, where they had any, and acquired a temperament of parsimony and suspicion.

Another tax was the *gabelle* or salt tax. This, like the *taille*, varied throughout France; in some provinces it was non-existent; in others it was light, elsewhere it was a harsh levy. The consumption of salt was greater than that today; for it served to preserve meat and fish; it was also used as a fertilizer; then as now it was given to cattle in order to minimize the risk of disease. The French Government made salt a monopoly, like tobacco; a certain minimum amount had to be taken for household use, and a coarser variety was supplied for other purposes; it was the duty of a large army of inspectors (employed by the capitalists who farmed the tax) to see that the minimum was taken; that the coarser and cheaper variety was not used as a substitute for the finer; that salt was not made secretly from brine. By reference to his books and inspection of a man's household and cattle, a competent inspector could determine whether there was any abuse of the regulations; for example, suppose the books showed that only the minimum had been taken, and the cattle were found to be diseased, then the one fact explained the other, and everything was in order; but suppose only the minimum quantity and a herd of healthy cattle (as shown by examination of their hides), then one of two things might have happened; the householder must have made his own salt, or he had smuggled it from a province where it was not so expensive. Further complications were introduced when the Government poisoned the salt intended for fertilizing so that it could not be used for men or cattle; a slightly different policy was that of mixing sand with the salt purchased for cattle, so that it was useless for the household; but there was sometimes such a high proportion of sand as to cause the death of the animals to which it was administered. The privileged were exempt from this levy, which was enforced by penalties extending to life and limb.

In addition to the *taille* and the *gabelle* there were other taxes such as. the *aides*, levied mainly on wine; a tax on tobacco; the profits from the monopoly of the post; and a tax on legal documents. There was a large revenue from the royal demesne; there were also the customs, levied not only at the ports but at the passage of goods through towns and provinces. If produce had to be sent for a considerable distance by inland transport, the customs and tolls levied thereon might be considerably more than the total value of the goods. In this way, therefore, some of the taxes of the *Ancien Régime* were direct hindrances to trade and commerce.

Such were the normal means of raising revenue. Among the extraordinary expedients to which resort might be made were these. First, and simplest of all, debt repudiation. This was done several times with the *rentiers*. Another, but more heroic measure, was to pawn the royal plate. A third was to invite subscriptions for a Tontine. This device was introduced into France early in Louis's reign by an Italian named Tonti. His scheme was simple. Lenders to the Government were arranged in groups according to age; and as members of each group died off the survivors might have either an increased annuity or, where annuities were not part of the scheme, a better prospect of obtaining all the stakes by sole survivorship. A gamble in longevity, the scheme provided an immediate supply of ready money to the Treasury; and if, as sometimes happened, the lenders invested on behalf of children, then the date of repayment was delayed as long as possible. This scheme was frequently incorporated into issues of *rentes*. A fourth, and more ancient device was to debase the coinage; a fifth was to compel privileged corporations such as the guilds to pay heavily for the confirmation of their privileges; a sixth was to sell patents of nobility, or enforce payment from those who had usurped such titles. Finally, there was the extraordinary expedient of creating new offices, or subdividing old ones, or threatening to do one or other of these things, and obtaining money either from carrying out the threat or withdrawing it. About 4,000 new offices were created in the later years of the reign, many of which were forfeited at the beginning of the next; and so in 1715 few towns were without their grand hereditary criers of funerals, or sworn vendors of suet, or inspectors of perruques.

The extended use of these exceptional methods, together with the steady increase in war expenditure necessitated by the War of the Spanish Succession, effected a revolution in French society; for there was brought into existence a new and powerful class, mostly of humble origin but everywhere linked, by marriage or interest with the Court and the nobility. There were first of all the tax-farmers such as Le Riche and Romanet whose fortunes may be estimated from the fact that, between 1689 and 1697, of the 350 million livres[1] brought into the Treasury from taxation, the farmers had one hundred millions. This was exceptional; normally, the farmer expected to gain at least 15 per cent. gross profit; and from this he had to deduct the bribes paid to those at Court who had helped him to secure the contract. More unscrupulous were the army contractors and dealers in munitions, of which the brothers Paris are examples; these men made large fortunes; more honest were the private bankers such as Bernard and Hoggers who obtained wealth without losing esteem; other means of making money were card-sharping and coining; the first not unknown at Versailles, and the second occasionally practised by government officials.

But all wars are generally accompanied by drastic redistribution of wealth. Most characteristic of France in 1715 were a class known as the 'prospectors' (*les donneurs d'avis*). Their proposals were varied. One who suggested a tax on boots and shoes was sent to the Bastille; but others were more astute, as for example one named Lemaire, who undertook to create ten presidential offices in Parlement. He effected this by interviewing the right people; first, a financier, to secure an advance; then an abbé who knew a marquise. The marquise could get in touch with the Maréchal de Rochefort, who could bring the matter to a minister. At each stage a payment was made; the ten presidential chairs were set up and sold, and thus the *donneur d'avis* had brought off a successful speculation. There were many other lines of business: marriages between finance and nobility; military commissions; sale of crosses of Saint Louis;

[1] The livre was worth about 1s. 8d. in English money of the period.

liberation, by purchase, of men sent to the galleys; for these varieties of traffic there was a great hierarchy of agents, from the valets and chamber-women to the ministers and the dukes and peers. Louis XIV in all his glory was surrounded by middlemen and commission agents.

Thus finance helped to link the social classes, but the hybrids so propagated were insistent on the perpetuation of caste. Of the castes, the clergy had the greatest solidarity. Unlike the great ecclesiastics of the Germanic Empire, the French prelates were held in subordination to the Crown, and many of them were courtiers; in the provinces, some of them were treated as functionaries and gave their help in the suppression of Protestantism. Similar duties were sometimes imposed on the village *curés* who, as they were generally of humble origin, maintained a more intimate relationship with the peasants than was possible for the majority of the English parish clergy; moreover, at a time when there were few country schools, and illiteracy was general, the pulpit was the main instrument of both instruction and propaganda. It is a noteworthy fact that throughout the *Ancien Régime* the lower clergy did not incur the dislike with which the upper clergy were regarded. Indeed, the two often seemed to represent entirely opposed conceptions of Christianity; for while the curés shared their poverty with the husbandmen from whom they had to extract their tithe, the bishops were generally secular in spirit, uncompromising in temper, concerned either with promotion or the enforcement of their privileges; almost always distinguished by opposition to every measure which threatened, however remotely, to disturb an order of things so eminently favourable to their comfort and power. They were the strongest bulwark of privilege in French society. Official Christianity suffered further discredit from the large number of abbés who held *in commendam*. These abbés, though drawing the revenues of one or more benefices, were non-resident; some of them did not even know where their benefices were situated; and the lay character of their activities gave point to the criticisms of those who contended that the Church was little more than a means of providing revenues for men of birth or influence. In proportion as the nobility became impoverished, the higher ranks of the clergy became more exclusively recruited from its members.

In 1715 the clergy were almost equal in numbers to the nobility;

together they accounted for rather more than a quarter-of-a-million persons. The *noblesse d'épée* included the princes of the blood, the legitimized princes; the hereditary dukes and peers; the non-hereditary dukes; marquises, counts, and *écuyers*. Louis made considerable additions to their numbers, and between 1696 and 1711 he sold no less than 800 new titles of nobility. Unlike the English peerage, the French nobility had for the most part severed its connexion with the soil; they still drew services and revenues from land; but they were mostly non-resident; the more ambitious flocking to Paris and Versailles. Their immunities encouraged in some a natural tendency to homicide. As for those who were obliged to spend their lives on their estates, they were generally poor and despised; they were afraid of *Grands Jours*, or judicial investigation, such as had been conducted in Auvergne; for now they feared the King almost as much as they despised the peasant. The majority of them lived secluded lives, distinguishable only by armorial bearings and idleness from those of the husbandmen around them; at times this seclusion was intensified:

C'est un gentilhomme de Beauce
Qui se tient au lit quand on refait ses chausses.

The professions were part of an inferior nobility, the *Noblesse de Robe* and the *Noblesse Comitive*, consisting mainly of magistrates, lawyers, municipal councillors, doctors, and certain university professors. These men were organized in corporations, which might be a Parlement, or the Council of a municipality, or the Faculty of a University; like the clergy and nobility they were all insistent on their privileges; and while they were associated with certain advanced movements such as Jansenism and the rights of corporate institutions, they collectively acquired an increasing interest in the perpetuation of the existing order of things, and in this way they steadily sacrificed popular support. Their mingling of liberalism with reaction was to be strikingly illustrated in the eighteenth century; and it was characteristic that the Parlement which effected the expulsion of the Jesuits opposed the judicial reforms of Maupeou, and helped to ruin the work of Turgot. From this class were drawn some of the most enlightened men in France; witness Montesquieu, who was a magistrate of Bordeaux; but as a class the professions provided one more strand in the wrappings which held an antiquated system together. Montesquieu was the exception; the average may have approximated more closely to the young man of twenty-seven, whose appointment to a high administrative office was thus described by Madame de Sévigné:

I have seen him thousands of times and never once thought of him as a magistrate; but that is what he has become, by his reputation; moreover, at the cost of 14,000 francs he has bought all the experience necessary for supreme control of a sovereign body, the Chambre des Comptes of Nantes.

The great mass of the population, sometimes loosely designated the Third Estate, was composed of the smaller burgesses, craftsmen, *métayers*, and serfs. This classification implies a clearer differentiation than actually existed; for there were many part-time occupations; thus a peasant might work during the winter in one of the factories which Colbert had established; in many villages, especially in the north, agricultural work was supplemented by handicrafts; and throughout France, the unit of labour was not the individual but the family. In the towns, a close supervision was exercised by corporations such as the *jurandes*, which supervised workmanship, and helped to confine the exercise of crafts to a limited number of persons, so that a new-comer would find it extremely difficult to establish himself, and might be forcibly expelled. Coupled with this exclusiveness of the towns was their dependence on the executive. This was secured by an edict of 1692 which abolished their elective magistracies, and replaced them by mayors and assessors, nominated by the Crown. These offices were sold, and so there began a regular traffic in the purchase of franchises and perquisites, which, together with their indebtedness, helped to deprive the municipalities of whatever autonomy they had once possessed.

The smallest unit of administration was the village. It still retained some traces of communal organization; for the inhabitants held assemblies on Sundays, at which two representatives might be elected—the collector of the *taille* and the syndic, or treasurer and secretary for village affairs. But by 1715 these were somewhat pathetic survivals. To be chosen collector of the *taille* was often tantamount to a sentence of imprisonment; to be syndic was to incur the attentions of both *seigneur* and intendant. In 1702 an attempt was made to extend officialdom into the humblest quarters by creating the office of perpetual syndic and offering it for sale; but there were few tenders. Generally, the village was responsible for the support of the church and the *curé*, and (where it existed) the school; otherwise it was completely subjected to the rule of the *seigneur*; or, if on royal domain, to executive officials.

The village population included serfs and *métayers*; but of the former there were not more than about 140,000, to be found mainly in the eastern provinces. Their condition was that of a mitigated serfdom; they were *mainmortables;* that is, they had no freedom of bequest, and their holdings, where they did not revert to the lord, were transmitted to children living in community with them. Technically, this serfdom was attached not to the person but to the holding, and might therefore be transmitted by marriage to a free women. Far more numerous were the *métayers*, who were generally furnished with implements and cattle by the lord; in return for which they paid him a proportion of the yield. This proportion differed considerably; it might vary from a fifth to a half, and it might be paid partly in kind, and partly in money; moreover, the tenure might be on a short lease, or on a lease of such length that it amounted to freehold. In several parts of France there were a considerable number of such peasant proprietors; but ownership did not necessarily mean prosperity; for the holdings were small, and were often sub-divided; nor was the proprietor free from payments to his immediate overlord, whether the King, the Church or the *seigneur*. All classes of peasant had to pay the *taille*; they might be called on to make roads; or forced into military service, or have troops billeted on them; and what this meant may be inferred from the fact that, at the sight of a regiment a whole village might take to flight. Contemporary evidence points to the conclusion that the position of the peasant was precarious, impoverished, and despised.

In years of peace he could generally make just enough to support his family; indeed, his cultivation rarely rose above subsistence level: nor was there any encouragement to produce a surplus, because of the restrictions on transport and export, and because throughout the greater part of Louis's reign the price of corn remained low. Such conditions, just tolerable in peace, were made almost intolerable in war; and between 1689 and 1715 France enjoyed very few years of peace; with the result that famine and misery were the fate of the countryside during the later years of the reign. Nor were these consequences confined to the years immediately preceding 1715. Colbert had done little for French agriculture; the wars of Louis ruined it, and the result was the frequent recurrence of famine during the first half of the eighteenth century, in which there were more deaths from starvation than from wounds. Herein was the most obvious consequence of the policy pursued by Louis XIV. He drew without stint on the resources of his country; he engaged in war when the nation could afford it and when it could not afford it; and the cost fell most heavily on that class which, as it was at the basis of the system, had to endure the pressure from above of every other class:

Quel plaisir a-t-il depuis qu'il est au monde?
En-est-il un plus pauvre en la machine ronde?
Point de pain quelquefois et jamais de repos,
Sa femme, ses enfants, les soldats, les impôts,
Le créancier et la corvée
Lui font d'un malheureux la peinture achevée.[1]

Those contemporaries such as La Bruyère who went to the trouble of noticing what the peasant looked like, generally described him as haggard and emaciated, twisted with labour, and blackened with exposure; a leper from whom the spectator would usually turn his gaze. But even at its worst, the countryside was not always a place of gloom; for in the midst of its abject poverty there was often preserved that mother wit and frank interest in other people's affairs which still distinguishes the peasantry of the more remote corners of France. In the freemasonry of the highways and fields there was abundant opportunity for this curiosity and repartee; strangers meeting each other seldom passed in silence; solicitude for others was easily aroused, and if the peasant could offer no bread, he was seldom without his fund of worldly wisdom and advice. Men in rags might set up as sartorial critics; and the half-famished expounded unblushingly their convictions on the right conduct of life. Such at least was the kind of society which La Fontaine had in mind when he wrote his fable Le Meusnier, son fils et l'âne; an old story, now given a characteristically French setting. The miller and his son took their ass to the market in order to sell it. In the hope of keeping it in the best condition they tied its legs together and carried the animal; but this spectacle aroused the mirth of the first passer-by; and thereupon (acting upon somewhat sarcastic advice) the miller placed the ass on the ground and rode upon it. But this

[1] La Fontaine, Le Vieillard et la Mort.

did not please the next traveller whom they met; for he objected that the unfortunate youth was obliged to walk; whereupon the miller changed places with his son, only to incur even more pointed pleasantries from the third wayfarer, who insisted that age should come first and that therefore the youth must walk. In the hope of satisfying both schools of criticism, father and son mounted on the ass, and received the sharp reprimand of one who objected that the ass was grossly overladen. Then the two walked behind the ass, and so provided a good butt for the fifth critic, who ridiculed their folly in walking when they might ride. So everyone took his turn at solving this problem of the miller, the son, and the ass:

Quant à vous, suivez Mars, ou l'Amour ou le Prince,
Allez, venez, courez, demeurez en Province;
Prenez femme, abbaye, employ, gouvernement,
Les gens en parleront, ne'en doutez nullement.

8
Louis and the French Genius

No Maecenas ever exercised such an inclusive and exacting patronage as did Louis; for he controlled inspiration and policy alike with magisterial autocracy; and in the direction of both there was the same attention to detail. Pensions to men of genius were from year to year, and were tenable only during the production of satisfactory results; foreigners were invited to offer subsidized contributions; and even in hostile England, where there were known to be poets of repute, it was thought that recruits might be found for this literary campaign. The results were voluminous and varied. Dedications, panegyrics, odes, medals, and equestrian statues all attest the response to the appeal; for poets and painters alike the King's glory was often the set theme; historical research was of value in so far as it revealed the long process of evolution culminating in this greatness; and both publicist and preacher were encouraged to view the record of human striving from the pinnacle of the royal achievement. Artists might still go to the classical past for their models of expression; but not for their subject; for Louis was Jupiter, Apollo, Phœbus, Alexander, Augustus, and even the Sun itself; Versailles was an augmented Olympus; the minutest acts of the King were the subjects of artistic commemoration; for when he performed an act of charity, a medal perpetuated the fact; when he received a distinguished person at Court, the scene was recorded by the painters; the passage of the Rhine was eternalized in bas-relief; even his Revocation of the Edict of Nantes was signalized in art. With Molière, Lulli, and Quinault at command, he could secure the harmonizing of dramatic plot with music and verse; for his stage decoration he had Le Brun; for the innumerable engravings depicting his public acts there were Silvestre and Le Clerc; for the official diary of his doings there was Dangeau. There was an almost pagan richness about it all. But it coincided with a great efflorescence of the French genius; and though Louis rejected some of the best blooms, he yet gathered enough to make a very presentable bouquet.

Herein was the true civil service of his reign. Justice and finance might continue to be matters mainly of private enterprise, but literature and art were direct concerns of the State. As the crafts and trades were controlled by corporations and privileged companies, so the Academies gave authoritative rulings on all questions of inspiration; the French Academy having a supreme prerogative in matters of language and literature, while the Royal Academy of Painting and Sculpture formulated the rules of the graphic and plastic arts. This latter body, founded in 1648 and reconstituted by Colbert, served to liberate artists from guilds of workers and to erect them into a distinct corporation; the artist thereby became distinguished from the house-painter, and no longer did the sculptor have to conform with the regulations applying to stonemasons. But emancipation from one set of rules involved subordination to another; for the Academy had many conferences in which its members, after debate, agreed on certain fixed principles. In painting, Raphael and Poussin were the models; in statuary, it was the antique, notably the Laocoon; wherever nature differed from these, it was probably wrong. After 1664 Le Brun was the guiding spirit of the Academy, for he was its Rector; Colbert also displayed an active interest, and as its Protector he presided at annual meetings, when important general principles were formulated and registered with all the solemnity of Colbertian edicts. Thus was French art officialized.

A good result of this change was that the artist acquired a definite status, and his masterpieces were given a national importance such as they never had before and have not enjoyed since. But there were limitations in the type of art which Louis made popular. The first was that the Middle Ages were ignored; the Gothic was held up to scorn as barbarous, and this in a France so rich in medieval art; still more serious, there was little direct study of nature; and, though Poussin was in vogue, there was none of his personal and distinctive feeling for landscape. So horizons were contracted into mere suggestions of background, and everything was concentrated on the 'postures' of the figures in the foreground. In the continual search for allegory and classical allusion, men turned away from the sources of natural inspiration which lay at their doors; with results which can still be seen in the decorative canvases of the painters and the plates of the engravers. But nevertheless the art of Louis XIV was a true art because it embodied some of the characteristic conceptions of the age. It reflected an attitude of mind according to which one's own time represents the summit of achievement, consequent on a long period of preparation and inevitably preceding an age of decline. As men could not conceive the possibility of improvement in the future, they naturally looked to the classical past in order to find a parallel; hence a complete reincarnation of pagan mythology. At its worst, this attitude inspired merely the vapid and the trifling; at its best, it helped to make possible some of that stately quiescence so characteristic of the eighteenth century, and so sharply contrasted with the hot restlessness of today.

In these ways an attempt was made to subject the Muses to codes as strict and circumstantial as those which Colbert imposed on his workers. Even the poet was policed; his rhymes might no longer take a vagrant's chance, but must report regularly to the constable of reason:

Quelque sujet qu'on traite, ou plaisant ou sublime,
Que toujours le Bon Sens s'accorde avec la Rime.
L'un l'autre vainement ils semblent se hair;
La Rime est une esclave, et ne doit qu'obeir.
Lors qu'à la bien chercher d'abord on s'evertue,
L'esprit à la trouver aisément s'habitue.
Au joug de la raison sans peine elle fléchit,
Et loin de la gêsner, la sert et l'enrichit.
Mais lors qu'on la néglige, elle devient rebelle,
Et pour la ratraper, le sens court après elle.
Aimez donc la raison. Que toujours vos écrits
Empruntent d'elle seule et leur lustre et leur prix.

Boileau, the author of this quotation, did not have so close a connexion with Versailles as had Le Brun; but his influence on poetry was so great because the counsels of moderation and reasonableness which he laid down in his *Art Poetique* were unchallenged. Repose, balance, sequence; these were the qualities for which he sought in the products of inspiration; nor was he unreasonable in making these demands; for such qualities may often be found in the most characteristic expressions of the French genius, and they were amply illustrated in the literature of Louis XIV's reign. Their exercise appeared indeed to confer on that reign an atmosphere of finality and stability. But the same reign gave evidence of other and equally characteristic qualities; namely, originality and daring speculative inquiry, which threatened to undermine the foundation of Versailles as much as the other attributes served to strengthen it. Hence a mingling of assent and interrogation in the literature of *Le Grand Siècle*.

A similar dualism may be traced in the distinction between those who were patronized by the King and those who were not. In the first class, most of the greater names are to be found; these were Molière and Racine; coupled with them are Chapelain, Quinault, and Boileau. In this class also were many foreigners, notably German and Dutch, not all of them eminent; but there were no English. Almost as remarkable were the men who were not received at Versailles. Pascal, who died in 1662, would have been out of place there; Poussin preferred to live in Italy; Claude Lorrain appears to have been unknown at the French Court. Neither Madame de Sévigné, nor La Bruyère, nor La Fontaine owed anything to Versailles. Racine forfeited the royal favour because of his appeal on behalf of an oppressed peasantry; Fénelon was disgraced because of his expressed opinions, and was exiled to his archdiocese of Cambrai; the chemist Lémery, the optician Dolland, and the traveller Chardin were among the Protestants who left after the Revocation; Bayle and Saint-Évremond were among the earlier exiles. In 1667 Louis definitely forbade an oration in honour of the memory of Descartes. So Louis's association with the French genius was notable for its repudiations as for its recognitions; moreover, he survived all the great men with whom he was associated, and lived to see a France almost completely denuded of material and intellectual wealth.

The most famous of all who received the bounty of Louis was J. B. Molière, the greatest dramatist in French literature. His early life was a hard one; for, having chosen the stage in preference to the law, he toured the provinces with a company of actors. It is much to the credit of the King that he quickly recognized the genius of Molière, and royal patronage turned possible failure into success. His first well-known play, *Les Précieuses ridicules* (1659), is a satire on affectation, and perhaps the most famous burlesque inspired by ridicule of literary preciosity; it was specially appreciated by a nation which has always reacted strongly to literary sarcasm. But it was not a cruel sarcasm. A Juvenal or a Jeremiah might have indited a long tirade against social foibles and abuses; but Molière caricatured them with that balance between truth and over-emphasis which causes the victims to join in the laugh. The courtiers were not spared in *Les Fâcheux,* which ridiculed their somewhat inane conversation; *Tartuffe* (1667) was a tilt against religious hypocrisy, and led some contemporaries to the mistaken belief that it was an attack on religion itself. A safer subject for parody was the *bourgeoisie* of Paris; this was the motive of *Le Bourgeois gentilhomme,* one of the best of the satirical comedies of manners, and still one of the most popular of his plays. The *hobereaux* or unsocial country gentry were tackled in *Monsieur de Pourceaugnac;* while social life in the provinces (Angoulême) provided the theme of the lively *Comtesse d'Escarbagnas.* But Molière's humour was at its greatest when there was a background of tragedy. *Le Malade imaginaire* (1673) was composed when he was dying; it is an effective but kindly satire on the contemporary practices of the medical profession.

Molière is of supreme interest not only to the student of literature but to the student of history, because in his comedies one comes into contact with living creatures selected from almost every class and vocation. Only the King and the peasant are wanting to complete the picture; but the first was sacrosanct, and the second was left to that keen student of the humble—La Fontaine. Specially true to life are the dramatist's studies of the professions: the doctor, the notary, the magistrate; of those he had a minute knowledge, and they are always drawn with insight. As he had travelled from one end of the country to another, he knew intimately what was almost unknown to the educated inhabitant of Paris; namely, provincial France; and with his comedies in hand it is possible partly to repeople the whole country, and to reincarnate all the black-coat professions, the charlatans and quacks, dancing and fencing masters, actors and actresses. But experience never made him cynical. At heart, he was an idealist, and even an optimist; he disliked arti-ficiality and hypocrisy, and had a profound belief in natural instinct and nobility of character. It is not too fanciful to see his own picture in Alceste of *Le Misanthrope;* for Alceste experienced all the disillusionments inevitable when a noble and ingenuous character is pitted against an artificial and self-seeking society. Moreover, his keen perception of the incongruous was always linked with the qualities of humanity and humour. Of these two qualities, the sense of humour is generally a very late acquisition in national evolution; it is quite different from wit; for it consists primarily in a high standard of values, a sense of proportion, which enables its possessor to see everything including himself in true perspective. Its true converse is sometimes laughter, but never tears. Molière embodied French humour at its best.

A very different dramatist was Jean Racine, more than thirty years younger than Molière, one of the most notable products of the Port Royal schools. A laudatory ode secured for him an introduction to the royal favour in 1664 and he was given a pension; later he became historiographer royal. In character he was not built on the generous lines of his great contemporary; indeed, jealousy and ingratitude have served to cloud a reputation which might well have rivalled that of Corneille. Nor was it from contemporary manners that Racine derived his inspiration, but from the sacred and classical past; his field was therefore narrower than that of Molière; but within his selected limits he was more intense. At Port Royal des Champs he learned two things: an appreciation of the simple action and strong passion of Greek tragedy, and the habitude of analysing the emotions; these two influences caused him to think of life as an unequal contest wherein the human soul is the sport of incalculably great forces, a fragile barque which may at any moment be tossed against the rocks of destiny; hence for him a drama was a problem, not in the fate of the soul, but in the unloosening of the forces which precipitate that fate. Within this somewhat restricted sphere Racine was probably the greatest dramatist in modern literature; with Pascal, he was the most brilliant product of the Jansenist influence; but perhaps for these very reasons, he can be appreciated best in France, where these special conditions are most widely understood.

From his conception of drama as a problem in the interplay of fate and emotion, it follows that Racine was not incommoded by the unities of time and place; indeed the restrictions implied by these unities were essentials in his art; for he achieved his objects with the minimum of waste, each actor and incident being absolutely essential for the *dénouement*. Just as the individual was instantaneously transformed and directed into an entirely new path by the touch of irresistible Grace, so the complicated mechanism created by the interaction of human beings might be set going by some external event; and thereafter the drama leads remorselessly to its end. Rarely is the eye diverted by stage scenery; everything is concentrated on this gradual unfolding of inexorable purpose in the lives of men. Or rather in the lives of women; for Racine had an intuitive knowledge of the feminine heart; and all his greatest characters are women; such as Berenice, in the play of that name, whose tragedy was unrequited love; or Clytemnestra, whose love for her daughter Iphigenia dwarfs Agamemnon and the Greeks when that daughter is offered up as a sacrifice in *Iphigénie*; or Andromaque, who made an even greater sacrifice when she was carried off by Pyrrhus after the siege of Troy. In *Esther* this exalted conception of womanhood achieved its highest expression; for there a woman intercedes with her husband in order to save a whole race from extinction. Love, irresolution, sacrifice; these were the motives which he handled with the dexterity of genius; he could make emotion communicative; for the women in his auditories saw on his stage something of the domestic tragedies of which they themselves had experience; and all this in some of the finest poetry in the French language. Racine is the most French of all writers because his genius was most akin to the Greek.

Molière and Racine helped to make the Court of Versailles the most brilliant in modern history; more important they conferred distinction on a language which was fast becoming an essential part of intellectual equipment. But drama was only one of the many forms in which the genius of the French found expression. For example, there was a great moralist literature. To modern ears the adjective might seem derogatory; but it should be recalled that there was then a vast borderland between the domains of theology and human conduct, in which there were many explorers. Earlier in the century, preachers, philanthropists, and reformers such as Saint Francis of Sales, Saint Vincent de Paul, and the abbé Saint-Cyran had contributed to a renaissance of French catholicism; and something of this revived spirit can be traced in the reign of Louis XIV, when there was established a sharp antithesis between the strictness of the devout, and the libertinage of the fashionable; moreover, as nearly every great personage had his own confessor, and as greater specialization was introduced into the ministrations of the spiritual guides, there was developed what, for want of a better term, may be called a spiritual psychology. Within the Church there were the two extremes, the Jansenists and the Jesuits, between whom the inquirer might choose; but there were many intermediate shades; and almost every variety was provided for. This exploration of human character and conduct resulted in the discovery of an ideal type; the *honnête homme*; a mean between extremes; one who excels in all the arts that help to make life more happy; a man distinguished by solicitude for the welfare of others as for his own good name. This ideal was afterwards to find its personification in Montesquieu, who incarnated not so much *réputation* as *considération*, and won fame not by a single achievement, but by a sustained quality of life and character. In the reign of Louis XIV the *honnête homme* was taking shape not only in books, but in salons, notably in that of Madame de Sablé, where (owing perhaps to Jansenist influence) the qualities of primness and rectitude were chiefly in vogue.

One product of this salon was the Duc de la Rochefoucauld whose *Maximes*, first published in 1665, reduced human action to the motive of self-interest. They expressed in memorable and epigrammatic form the results of that self-analysis for which the Port Royalists were famous; but they lack the constructive elements to be found in such moralists as Pascal or Arnauld. Personal timidity, coupled with disillusionment, served to make the *Maximes* pungent, but this does not save them from aridity; they give only one side of the picture, and may be taken to represent the negative or sterile elements in the results achieved by the Jansenist method. There is a more constructive quality in the social portraits or *Caractères de notre siècle* (1688). Their author, La Bruyère, spent the earlier part of his career as a tutor in the family of the great Condé, and the extreme arrogance of that prince ensured that the more thoughtful of his dependants were driven to ponder deeply on the problems of human character. Like La Rochefoucauld, he suffered from disillusionment; but unlike his noble contemporary he was never driven to cynicism; for he thought that satire and criticism might serve a social purpose. In general, he was severe on the mighty and in sympathy with the weak; he condemned in unmeasured terms the idleness and viciousness to be found at times among the French nobility, and contrasted therewith the virtue and self-sacrifice of which the poorest were often capable. Hence a new and disturbing element in the literature of the century; new, because for many, birth was still the criterion of both character and ability; disturbing, because, if La Bruyère was right, then many inferiors were at least as good men as their superiors. It was a revolutionary doctrine long before the Revolution.

But La Bruyère was better known as a stylist than as a social reformer; and it is mainly for his contribution to French prose that he is honoured in literature. He had no great gift of insight, but he had a sense of construction and finish; hence he built up his characters in successive tiers; each giving sharper definition to its predecessor; and his language has that lapidary quality which comes from mature deliberation and methodical revision. More spontaneous and also more subtle than *Les Caractères* of La Bruyère are the Fables which La Fontaine began to publish in 1668. The fabulist, son of a guardian of woods and forests, was not a moralist in the strict sense of the word; indeed his life could not be described as a moral one; but in his studies of animal creation and adventure he portrayed human qualities with such delicacy and allusiveness as to earn for himself the title of *The Inimitable*. It is tempting to read some kind of symbolism into these Fables; to identify his lions with Louis XIV; or his asses, hardened to work and blows, with the peasants; nevertheless it is possible to assign to this disordered and poetic naturalist too great a measure of deliberate intention. His interests may have been more in nature than in morality. One theme, however, recurs with insistent regularity; it is that he is happiest who gives fewest hostages to fortune; or, in his words, who exposes least of himself to the teeth of the enemy. The enemy is most often the fox; the victims are those who have been charmed by his fluency and flattery. La Fontaine's Reynard is not a solitary prowler like the wolf; nor is he a quarrelsome creature like the dog; for he is continually trying to live down his bad reputation by evidences of good faith and sociability, and he would have been the first to sign a social contract in order that he might have a larger circle of acquaintance. He gives a brotherly kiss on the cheek before he implants his fangs in the neck. Possibly he représents acquisitive and highly-polished society preying on the simple-minded; the unequal struggle between hard circumstance and the yielding ingenuousness of the *honnête homme*.

A less enigmatic moralist was J. B. Bossuet, who was born of *bourgeois* parents at Dijon in 1627, and became Bishop of Condom in 1669 and of Meaux in 1681. His career and character were of monumental proportions; for he was a pillar of the Church; a stronghold of piety and learning; a rampart against heresy and innovation; the master of a majestic prose, divided into symmetrical perorations as by Corinthian pillars, a style reflecting a mind that was spacious, orderly, and lucid. There was some breadth even in his religious outlook. He corresponded with Leibnitz on a scheme for uniting the Catholic with the Lutheran churches; he was in sympathy with the Jansenists, though he did not commit himself to their views; but on the other hand, against Protestantism, Mysticism, and Ultramontanism he maintained a solid front. He was a Father of the Church, towering above vagaries and sects; exposing errors, winning converts, and expounding the truth in compositions of herculean force and magnitude. He alone reproached the monarch with his private conduct and escaped disgrace.

By the mere enumeration of the topics on which he discoursed, it is possible to realize how Bossuet explored almost every field of human thought as known in the later seventeenth century. These subjects included patristic studies; biblical interpretation; abstract theology; the reinterpretation of Cartesian metaphysics; the science of logic; political theory; national history and universal history. As a moralist he is seen at his best in his sermons and correspondence; in at least one branch of literature, the *Oraison Funèbre* or obituary sermon, his supremacy is unchallenged; for he was at his best when contrasting the impermanence of earthly glory with the eternity of the spirit. To him, the essential thing in Christianity was the supernatural, as revealed in the Scriptures and expounded by the Fathers; all knowledge was therefore subordinated to this central doctrine; everywhere definition and dogma are substituted for speculation or doubt. He stood high in the esteem of Louis, whom he resembled in his intellectual expansiveness and confidence; both men had a natural distrust of whatever was outside their understanding; the one explained God's purpose for humanity, while the other appeared to illustrate these Divine intentions as did no other king.

For an adequate comment on Bossuet there would be needed not a paragraph but an encyclopaedia. Among the best known of his writings is the *Histoire des variations des Églises Protestantes*, where he adduced the well-known argument that Protestantism was completely discredited by the number of warring sects into which it had degenerated; even better known is the book which he compiled in 1670 for his pupil, the Dauphin, the *Discours sur l'histoire universelle*, one of the earliest and most successful abridgments of human history, based on a conception which has still some vogue—that of the essential unity of all history. Bossuet was also before his time in his recognition of the influence of climate and environment on national evolution. The *Universal History* was so planned as to enable the reader to see, as on a map, the relative position of contemporary Europe; it was an intelligent linking together of particular histories, intended to show the working of Divine purpose in the destinies of many peoples, but more especially of the Jews. Its starting-point was the Creation (4004 B.C.), which was speedily followed by the increase of the human species: 'the earth began to be populated and crimes to increase'. This was the first epoch, and was followed by the Deluge; then there was the 'Vocation of Abraham', succeeded by 'Moses and the Written Law'. Following an excursion to Troy, a return was made to sacred history in 'Solomon, or the completion of the Temple'; and after diversions to Romulus, Cyrus, and Scipio the age of Christ was at last reached; completed by the ages of Constantine and Charlemagne, and, finally by that of Louis XIV. It was indeed an imposing panorama; a picturesque delineation of progress and purposefulness. One moral lesson predominated: how the fortunes of God's chosen people varied with their piety. Virtue was rewarded with prosperity, and sin was punished by disaster. It was an apt lesson for a Bourbon prince; for were not his people a chosen race?

Bossuet was a great controversialist; and as he did not spare heretics, so he anathematized every Catholic aberration from the true faith. Perhaps the most notable of the controversies in which he was involved was that with Fénelon on the subject of mysticism and Madame Guyon; this controversy was a bitter one, because it brought out all the forthcoming qualities in Bossuet's temperament. Madame Guyon was a seer; today she would have been classed as a spiritualistic medium; she had visions, and wrote messages inspired by a power external to herself. She believed in a doctrine of 'pure love', according to which it was possible, by cultivation of the emotions, to assimilate one's personality with the divine in a unison so perfect that all earthly passions and needs were eliminated. This conception is not unknown in oriental mysticism; it may have come to France through Spain; indeed, Madame Guyon's absolute surrender of the personality produced a state not unlike the Nirvana of the Eastern philosophers. Fénelon was interested in her revelations, and by befriending her he associated himself to some extent with her views; to Bossuet, however, these views seemed as pernicious as Protestantism, because their application led to neglect of all the Christian duties enjoined by the Church. The result was a somewhat acrimonious correspondence; in addition, both ecclesiastics wrote books intended to show the proper purposes of Mysticism; but Fénelon had the worst of it. So the doctrine of 'pure love' was ruled out of court; and one more victory was achieved for the sense of duty which, more than anything else, inspired the moralizings of Bossuet and the conduct of Louis.

The dualism represented by Bossuet and Fénelon provides illustration of the rich variety of genius with which the King came into contact. François de Salignac de Lamothe-Fénelon was born of a poor but noble family in 1651. He was a meridional and an aristocrat, as Bossuet was a *bourgeois* and a townsman. He was trained for the Church, and one of the earliest duties entrusted to him was that of instructing the New Catholics, or converted Huguenots in Saintonge, for which he was specially qualified by his tact and sympathy; moreover, he knew how highly specialized is the vocation of teaching, and how dependent for success on the temperament of the teacher. His principles of pedagogy were enunciated in his *Traité de l'éducation des filles*, one of his earliest writings; here he showed that he was somewhat in advance of his times. In place of the older ideal which made of education a device for repressing natural inclination and replacing it by book learning, he substituted a method intended to train the intelligence by the encouragement of interests. He thought it natural that children should ask questions and expedient that they should be answered; pleasure, he considered, might not necessarily be an evil, but rather a useful stimulus. For prodigies he had no sympathy. Even more novel was his belief, expounded elsewhere, that a knowledge of trade and commerce might be useful for a prince. Instead of the composition of formal themes in Latin, he encouraged the more general use of the vernacular and even prescribed the transcription into prose of La

E

Fontaine's verse. These heterodoxies are sharply contrasted with the traditionalism of Bossuet as educator.

On the advice of Madame de Maintenon, Fénelon was chosen to be preceptor of the Dauphin's eldest son, the Duke of Burgundy; and seldom has a prince had such an instructor. The pupil responded generously to the efforts of his tutor, and by his character and attainments he reflected credit on entirely new methods and principles. As Bossuet had written his *Universal History* for the father, so Fénelon wrote *Télémaque* for the son; the one book is a narrative of indubitable fact, the other is a mixture of allegory, allusion, and romance. For his services he was appointed Archbishop of Cambrai in 1694; but he did not preserve the royal favour for long. A servant purloined the manuscript of *Télémaque* and published it (1699), thereby making public what were considered to be veiled allusions to the rule of Louis; still worse, his *Explication des maximes des saints*, wherein he defended himself and Madame Guyon against the strictures of Bossuet, was condemned by the Papacy in 1699, and so the Archbishop was in double disgrace. On the death of the Duke of Burgundy in 1712 a number of his tutor's manuscripts were found among the Duke's papers; these were destroyed by order of the King. In the retirement of his archdiocese Fénelon preserved his solid reputation for meekness and sanctity; he devoted a large portion of his revenues to works of charity; he succoured refugees and the wounded when Cambrai was the scene of hostilities during the Spanish Succession War; and his palace was a place of resort for distinguished Frenchmen and foreigners. He died in 1715.

As critic of contemporary institutions Fénelon shows a striking liberalism of outlook, coupled with an unfailing optimism. In his *Traité de l'existence de Dieu* he sought for the proofs of God's existence not in tradition nor in revelation, but in final causes; in the *Explication des maximes des saints*, he expressed his appreciation of the rare and sublimated piety which transcends reason and annihilates self. Better known is his *Adventures de Télémaque* which, like *Gulliver's Travels*, can be read in childhood for the story and in maturity for the symbolism; it is a medley of fact and fiction, morality and politics, classical reminiscence and novel ideas. Two types of republic are described; one, the Betic, is intended for a pastoral people; the other, that of Salente, for an agricultural population. The first is fabulous and fantastic, a reminiscence of Arcadia; but the second has more application to historical conditions, because it appears to present such a deliberate contrast with the State as personified by Louis XIV. The ideals pursued in the republic of Salente are peace and abundance; everyone was engaged in the cultivation of the soil; the object of the legislator was to secure a regular increase of population in proportion to the development of agriculture; and the two evils definitely avoided were war and excessive taxation. In these views it is not too fanciful to see an anticipation of the doctrines of the eighteenth-century Physiocrats. Fénelon's ideal state was an aristocracy, social rank being clearly evidenced by dress, occupation, and privilege, where birth was accepted as the one distinction most likely to be respected by all; but these social castes were unlike those of Versailles, because they were inseparably linked with heredity and involved duties as well as rights. Fénelon thought that an absolutism is based on artificial conditions, which may easily be upset by a slight change; whereas an aristocracy is more stable, and collectively is better able to resist change or upheaval. It may be doubted, however, whether the alternative thus proposed was a practicable one; indeed historical experience proves that the rule of a strong king is always preferable to that of a horde of nobility.

Elsewhere the Archbishop was even more explicit in his criticism of Louis XIV. In his *Examen de conscience sur les devoirs de la royauté* (drawn up for the Duke of Burgundy) he condemned thirst of glory in kings and libertinage in their Courts; even more, he called in question the accepted conception of heroism by contrasting the fate of a famished beggar who steals a pistole with that of the hero who robs a neighbouring state of its independence; indeed, he noted how human nature is quick to condone robbery and violence, provided they are on a sufficiently large scale. There are magistrates to punish those who injure the individual, and poets to sing the praises of those who injure millions; such were the extraordinary doctrines of this preceptor of princes. Equally unorthodox was his *Mémoire* on the condition of France in 1710, a pamphlet depicting the misery produced by the almost ceaseless wars of the King, as illustrated within his own diocese. He compared the constitution of France to an old, broken-down machine, which continued to work as by a miracle and must necessarily break down at the first shock; and he thought that the economic distress everywhere prevalent was the most adequate commentary on the King's rule by divine right. Some of his statements provide interesting anticipations; thus, 'it should not be all for one, but one for the happiness of all'; 'A king should be all-powerful for good; but he should have his hands tied against evil'; and 'The king is no more than a man of the people, and is worthy of his crown only in so far as he devotes himself to the public good'. It is not difficult to understand why the Archbishop was forbidden access to Versailles.

Grace, elegance, lightness of fancy, love of novelty, independence of judgment; these are some of the qualities which distinguish Fénelon among his contemporaries, and serve to provide contrast with the majestic conviction and torrential force of Bossuet. It is characteristic that Louis found his high-priest in the *bourgeois* Bossuet and his critic in the aristocratic Fénelon; for it was in the middle classes that the old French monarchy had its strongest support. Of the humourless and pietistic France represented by Louis XIV Bossuet is the true exponent; but if one seeks for the more adventurous qualities of the race; for the allusiveness and irony of its language, and the sustained fertility of its thought, one must turn to Fénelon who, though not of Versailles, was of France.

This psychological interest in human character, so typical of French classicism, may be seen also though less directly in the Memoirs, in which seventeenth-century France was so rich. Movements such as the Fronde were followed by a great harvest of these personal revelations; in fact, most of the prominent actors in that episode recorded their personal contribution to the making of history. It was an essential of Louis's rule that opportunity for such individual contribution was diminished; accordingly, the Memoirs compiled in his reign have for their central themes the doings at Versailles, or the acts of the King. The most faithful record of these things is the *Journal* of Dangeau, which Saint-Simon afterwards used for his Memoirs. Several women who, had they lived fifty years later, might have presided over *salons*, acquired some reputation, or notoriety, by the writing of their *Mémoires*; these include Madame de Caylus, Madame de La Fayette, and Mademoiselle de Montpensier who, having played a great part in the Fronde, continued to be a source of disquietude and even romance under the domination of Versailles. Of more general interest are the *Mémoires sur les Grands Jours d'Auvergne*, by Esprit Fléchier, the most valuable source of information for the history of provincial France. Primarily a record of the judicial investigations into the misdeeds of the nobility of Auvergne (1665–6), this book gives an unimpassioned record of the iniquitous conduct of the *seigneurs* in regard to their dependants; it contains also an indictment of the secularism and indifference of the upper clergy. Even the *bourgeoisie* were not spared; for, according to Fléchier, they were either aping the nobility or in alliance with them. So far as these *Mémoires* were written on behalf of any class, it is the peasants; and the book provides from personal experience many illustrations of the social types of society which incurred the indictment of La Bruyère. Its details, many of them unquotable, enable the reader to pierce, at a solitary point, through the thin crust on which the fabric of the *Ancien Régime* was imposed.

But Fléchier's Memoirs were quite exceptional; for usually the memorialist was concerned to depict life in high society as it revolved round the author. This is true of the best known of all the Memoirs relating to the period, those of the duc de Saint-Simon. Son of one of Louis XIII's favourites, Saint-Simon was brought up to contrast the merits of the *ducs et pairs* with the self-seeking of the new nobility; and as the father was embittered by loss of influence, so the son was chagrined by his failure to secure promotion in the army, a failure due to his own insubordination. So there is a certain rancour in his Memoirs; not the rancour of an able man who has suffered disillusionment, but rather that of a mediocre man who had never risen to the height for which his birth seemed to qualify him. He sets out to be impartial; but he interprets everything and everybody according as they conform to the standards of the dukes and peers; often his character-sketches are merely intended to satisfy a desire for revenge; at times his Memoirs degenerate into a pane-gyric of himself and his family; his style is often involved and clumsy. But with all this, he did have a power of vivid portrait painting; indeed, nowhere else can be found such a life-like gallery as that which is presented in his pages. His judgements are sometimes unjust, but always memorable; witness that of the Duke of Bur-gundy:

He was born a terror, and in childhood he made people tremble; hard and revengeful, even to the most passionate extremes and towards inanimate things; endowed with a furious impetuosity; unable to suffer the least resistance without going off into transports which were enough to make spectators think he would break everything in his interior; obstinate to excess; seeking every kind of sensual experience; given up to every passion, and carried away by every pleasure.

More balanced is his sketch of Fénelon:

This prelate was a tall, thin man; well-made, pale and long-nosed; his eyes appeared to emit fire and energy like a torrent; his physiognomy was such as I have never seen in any other man; and, once seen, it was not easily forgotten. His features seemed to imply contraries, but they all harmonized; they expressed gravity and gallantry, the serious and the gay, revealing alike the savant, the bishop and the great *seigneur*. Most pronounced of all was the impression of delicacy, grace, decorum, and above all nobility. It needed an effort to stop looking at him.

This rings more true to life; in the original it is one of the many gems to be quarried from the literary excavations which Saint-Simon termed Memoirs.

More valuable, because more spontaneous, is the epistolary correspondence of the period. Almost all the great personages of the time wrote letters; and these, even where they do not possess literary quality, may be of interest for the light they throw on social conventions, or still more, they may reveal an exchange of ideas. That letter-writing is now a lost art may be due to the advantages of quick communication; or to the multiplicity of books and newspapers, or to the haste with which modern life is lived; but in the seventeenth century men welcomed an epistle for its information, and readily resorted to it as a record of experience. The greatest of the letter-writers, Madame de Sévigné, lived only on the fringes of the Court, but she had an interesting circle of acquaintance nevertheless.

Marie de Rabutin Chantal, born in 1626, was married at the age of eighteen to the Marquis de Sévigné, who seven years later was killed in a duel. The widow devoted herself to the education of her two children, her affection meeting with a warm response from the daughter who, in 1669, married M. de Grignan; within a few years the bridegroom was appointed to an administrative post in Provence, a great distance in those days from the maternal home in Brittany. This enforced separation deeply affected the mother; accordingly, she found some consolation in assiduous letter-writing to her daughter. Such was the apparently commonplace inspiration of the *Lettres*. At a time when the littérateurs were handling the grand subjects in the grand manner, this sociable and cultured widow was using her pen as a consolation for sorrow; and as she wished by regular correspondence to maintain some continuity of life and sentiment with her absent child, so she wrote convincingly and eagerly of those little things which make up such a large portion of human existence. Occasionally her maternal affection breaks through the gossip, as when she writes:

J'ai soupé avec Dangeau chez Madame de Coulanges; nous parlâmes *extrêmement* de vous.

But her feelings are generally kept under control; and in these words she expounds her philosophy of life.

Ma fille, il faut aimer pendant la vie, comme vous faites, la rendre douce et agréable, ne point noyer d'amertume et combler de douleur ceux qui nous aiment; il est trop tard de changer quand on expire.

These letters brought something new into literature. Many women of the Renaissance excelled in the writing of Latin or Greek; Queen Elizabeth might well have won a university prize for her Latin prose; but these accomplishments have little opportunity for the exercise of that feminine grace which may be found on almost every page that Madame de Sévigné wrote. She was by no means the first woman writer in France; but she was the first mother of a family to make her affairs of interest to posterity by writing about them; she was a woman and a mother before she was a writer. Man may be the profound thinker; but the woman is sometimes the more intuitive observer; Madame de Sévigné, it is true, did not penetrate very deeply, but her gaze covered a wide horizon, and her quick perception enabled her to understand, where a man would be unsympathetic. Hence she records many incidents to which only a woman can do full justice; witness her description of the scene at Versailles in December, 1670, when Louis forbade the marriage of Mademoiselle de Montpensier with M. de Lauzun:

M. de Lauzun received the command with all the respect, submission, fortitude and despair which such a great calamity entailed. As for Mademoiselle, following her usual practice, she burst out into violent cries, groans and sobs; and all day she has kept to bed, where she is on a soup diet.

The last detail is specially feminine. Better known is her description of a performance of Racine's *Esther* at Saint Cyr in February, 1689, which was staged by the young ladies of good birth maintained at the charge of Madame de Maintenon:

I can hardly describe to you the beauty of this drama; it is such a perfect harmony of melody, poetry and song that nothing is wanting to its perfection; the girls who act kings and great personages seem expressly made for the part; one's attention is on it all the time, and the only regret is to see it end. Everything in it is simple and natural, sublime and appealing; its faithfulness to bible narrative commands respect; all the airs are well matched to the words, which as they are taken from the Psalms and the Book of Wisdom have an appeal which one can scarcely resist without tears. The close attention and appreciation with which this piece was followed are proof of its fame. I was charmed; so was the marshal of Bellefonds, who went up to the King and told him how much he had enjoyed it, and how he was placed next to a lady worthy of the honour of seeing *Esther*. The King came to our places, and turning to me he said: 'Madame, I am assured that you appreciate it.' I replied: 'Sire, I am thrilled; my feelings cannot be expressed in words.' His Majesty then said, 'Racine has plenty of *esprit*'; to which I answered, 'Sire, he has indeed; but in truth these young persons have some too; for they throw themselves into the subject as if they were born for it.' 'Ah, as for that,' he replied, 'it is quite true.' With that the King walked off, leaving me an object of envy; as I was the only new-comer, and the King had been glad to notice that my admiration was sincere and undemonstrative.

The above passage reveals another characteristic of Madame de Sévigné—her deep fund of sentiment. It is true that she was not profoundly moved by the sights which she saw in the fields of Brittany—peasants on their knees before the soldiery; nor did she express more than a passing regret for the wretches who were hanged at Rennes after the Breton risings of 1675; but within certain limits she was extremely impressionable. She wept on hearing Lulli's music; she loved evening walks and she wrote of the 'strange temptation' of moonlight. These were unusual things in an age when civilization was somewhat artificial and conventional, and few men had yet acquired a love for natural environment. There was little depth in Madame de Sévigné, and less humour; but there is much of that *sensibility*, which was to find its most complete expression in the next century.

A study of French genius in this period would be incomplete without a reference to the exiles. Pre-eminent among these were Bayle and Saint-Évremond.

Pierre Bayle was born in 1647, in the province of Foix. In youth he was induced by the Jesuits to abjure his Protestantism; but he returned to his original faith, which he afterwards exchanged for Deism and a supreme distrust of all established forms of religion. In 1675 he was appointed to a professorship of philosophy at Sedan; but in 1681, with the suppression of the Protestant academies, he was obliged to leave France, and took up a similar appointment at Rotterdam. There he came into contact with Huguenot exiles; but the extreme latitude of his religious opinions alienated him from the French Protestants, who publicly repudiated him as an agnostic. Bayle's position was therefore a solitary one; added to this was an element of bitterness; for his brother had died a victim of religious persecution. In the campaign which he directed against obscurantism and bigotry he anticipated Voltaire; but he employed different weapons. He had no great gifts of style; he was a master of neither sarcasm nor irony; but he believed in the power of knowledge and criticism, and that by the substance of the one and the spirit of the other the whole edifice of ecclesiastical tyranny would be undermined.

His writings are inspired by these two main purposes; to apply rigid tests to whatever was most implicitly accepted, and to make available for the average inexpert reader some of the results achieved by the great band of researchers and scientists which was then engaged in the investigation of the secrets of nature. He was not the first French sceptic; indeed, an old tradition of indifference or even unbelief could be traced right back to Montaigne; but whereas the exponents of this tradition often disarmed their opponents by raillery or buffoonery, Bayle presented a naked blade at the heart of the enemy. He was probably an agnostic or deist rather than an atheist; what caused the accusation of atheism was his contention that piety may often be coupled with immorality, and that a man devoid of religious beliefs may nevertheless be a good man. He thus severed ethics altogether from religion. It was the appearance of what was possibly Halley's comet which first prompted him to express these views; for in his *Pensées diverses sur les comètes* (1682) he proclaimed that celestial phenomena have no direct connexion with human affairs, and that a community of infidels might, in its conduct, exemplify a high standard of morals; two novel views, such as could have been expounded publicly only in the comparative freedom of Holland. This argument from the indifference of the skies was indeed a new line of attack on the divine right by which kings and clergy ruled.

In 1684 he founded a journal named *Nouvelles de la république de lettres*; a popular review, intended to provide information about important discoveries, and to keep the reader informed of all that was afoot in the realms of literature and learning; in purpose and subject matter it was not unlike an earlier publication—the *Philosophical Transactions*—edited by one of the first secretaries of the English Royal Society. Most characteristic of all was his *Dictionnaire historique et critique*, of which the first edition appeared in 1697. This work was primarily intended to correct a similar dictionary which had appeared more than twenty years before, that of the abbé Moréri; and its object was an unusual one; namely, to re-interpret, in terms of the new and more critical standards, the records of ancient and modern civilization. For this purpose the method of short biographies was adopted, many of them coloured by the scepticism which had already given such offence to his fellow-refugees. Its information is mostly obsolete now; but it must have been a stimulating source for all who sought a record of the past uncoloured by theological assumptions. Its keynote was that there can be no prescription against the truth; that errors are none the better for being old; that, in an age of reason religion is discredited by adherence to dogmas demonstrably false. The *Dictionary* was therefore no mere piece of religious polemic; it was not Catholicism alone that was in question, but all the Christian faiths; and so it is not surprising that when in the middle years of the eighteenth century the *Encyclopaedia* came to be planned a model was found in the work of Bayle.

In these ways Bayle helped to discredit not religion but the excesses of religious professionalism; and less directly, he attacked the whole social and political system represented by the personal rule of Louis XIV. But not all the exiles were hostile to the King; as witness Charles de Saint-Denis, seigneur de Saint-Évremond, who was obliged to leave France in 1661 because of some uncomplimentary remarks about the Treaty of the Pyrenees. Hitherto, he had defended the royal cause with his sword and his pen; and he had distinguished himself at the battles of Rocroi and Nördlingen; now he was forced to devote himself wholly to literature; and in the comparative freedom of the English Court he found an atmosphere congenial to his qualities of sarcasm and irony. He lived in England until his death in 1703, and had the remarkable distinction that he was favoured and pensioned by both Charles II and William III. He therefore had a genius for adaptation to environment.

As a conversationalist Saint-Évremond had abundant opportunity at Charles's Court, where also he had the society of women, to whom he acknowledges his debt; indeed, he helped to acclimatize a certain element which, for want of a better word, might be called femininity. Hitherto, the literature of concerted effort, as distinguished from that of inspiration, had been the product mainly of the study; it often gave expression to men driven in upon themselves; pedantry and virulence sometimes accounted for its inception. Saint-Évremond was one of those who helped to make it a thing of the drawing-room; the product not of solitude, but of polite intercourse; more ephemeral, but more urbane; the expression of a society which admitted refining influences, and veiled the serious or the commonplace in the epigrammatic and the allusive. Thus was engendered a variegation of the *honnête homme*; a new species of human being, courteous, witty, and unenthusiastic about the more solid things of life. For the training of this type Saint-Évremond rejected the study of theology and mathematics; in their place he substituted ethics (*morale*), politics and literature (*belles lettres*). The first, as it is the product of reason, teaches one to govern the passions; the second, being concerned with man in the state of society, trains the social aptitudes; while the third is the flower of that society, flourishing best where there is opportunity for polite conversation. So the Muses were transformed from domineering viragoes into submissive handmaidens; and they might now be admitted into the best society; but only on probation. There must be no more fits of frenzy; for these would not accord with the maxims of *la morale*.

It may be inferred therefore that Saint-Évremond excelled more in criticism than in creation; indeed it is true to say that modern literary criticism dates from him. Men still consulted Longinus or Aristotle for the laws of taste; but in the essays of this exiled Frenchman they might find examples of the *causerie*, the intimate, informal talk; never didactic nor dogmatic, but revelling in those minuter shades which help to make it a highly-specialized art. The same method was admirably illustrated by Dryden, in the short, brilliant essays which he prefixed to many of his plays. There are notable examples in Saint-Évremond. His criticisms might sometimes have been expressed more tersely; often he lingered over a subtle distinction, elaborating it, as in the course of conversation, in order that full justice might be done to the particular degree of discrimination which he had in mind. In this way was developed a secondary branch of literature—that of appreciation. One might have very little to say; but it might be said so well that one could not wish it unsaid.

Saint-Évremond turned his hand to many literary forms, in none of which did he rise to any great heights; for while his presence would be sufficient to guarantee the success of a literary salon, his attendance on the Muses was generally perfunctory. Nevertheless he anticipated what some of his successors have brought to fruition. Thus, in his historical sketches he was not content merely to retail a list of facts; he noted customs; he perceived the reaction of environment on character; and he had a feeling for what was afterwards called 'the spirit of the age'. This is true of his short studies of Roman history, where he shows an interest in the psychology of his characters, most of which are so delineated that they are neither wholly good nor bad, but are complicated studies of the infinite gradations between greatness and pettiness to be found in the living man. In this way Saint-Évremond helped to break down the formalism to be found in many of the older histories; and by connecting the study with the salon, he helped to make the man-of-letters more facile, more intimate, and therefore more likely to appeal to an audience distinguished for culture rather than scholarship. He was an unpaid and unacknowledged ambassador of French civilization abroad.

Bayle and Saint-Évremond are illustrations of the diffusion of French genius in foreign lands, a diffusion which helped to spread a knowledge and appreciation of the French language. There can be little doubt that, by its sheer magnificence and preponderance, Louis's reign was responsible for the propagation in Europe of the language of Versailles. It was so in diplomacy; for French came to displace Latin as the language of treaties, and its idiom came to be an essential element in the training of ambassadors; it was so also in education, for French began to be considered an essential part of a gentleman's education. In consequence of this, English, and to a lesser extent German, were rendered more flexible means of literary expression; not so much by the incorporation of new words or phrases, as by the adaptation, in these languages of the ironical, the elusive, and all the secondary modes of expression which may be found at their best in good French prose. The change may be noted by comparing the language of two men who were very nearly contemporary—Bunyan and Dryden. The one writes with Saxon directness and simplicity; the other composes both agreeably and innocuously; and sometimes his prose reads as if it had been translated from the French. It was perhaps fortunate that the native idiom underwent this change; because as administration became more specialized, and interest in politics more national, there was needed a less downright and more accommodating mode of expression; and in the greater stress of public life experience was suggesting that a phrase may sometimes be of value in proportion as it is non-committal, or anodyne; for just as the most complicated machinery moves easily with the help of a lubricant, so a single piece of grit may cause it to stop. The French influence may have helped to increase the proportion of lubricant in the communications of the English-speaking peoples.

These selected examples are sufficient to attest the pre-eminence of Louis's reign in the history of French thought, and help to account for the veneration with which Frenchmen, including even Voltaire, regarded the hegemony of Versailles in genius as in policy. Versailles created a cult of French literature, and by making it national removed the older subservience to foreign models. But just as there was a clear distinction between those who acquiesced in and those who questioned the system of which the King was the exponent, so the reign itself falls into two distinct parts; one brilliant and fruitful, the other singularly lacking in either promise or achievement. The dividing line is the year 1689 when Louis embarked on the war known as the War of the League of Augsburg, by which date Molière was dead, and though Racine was to survive ten years, he produced in that period only one notable play—*Athalie* (1691)— which proved a failure. With the War of the Spanish Succession Versailles lost much of the gaiety and sparkle of earlier years, and France became more sombre and purposeful; a France almost totally devoid of fancy or wit. There was disillusionment; there was also supreme confidence in the future not only of France but of humanity. Of this chastened but wider outlook two examples may be cited—Fontenelle and Saint-Pierre.

Le Bovier de Fontenelle was born at Rouen in 1657 and died in 1757. There were few idle years in the century allotted to him; he was prudent and unimpressionable, and his gift of permanent equilibrium served him well amid the many subjects and interests over which he gyrated. He had no enthusiasms; he thought all things were possible; but he had a supreme belief in progress and in science. His post of secretary of the Academy of Sciences (1699–1737) served to keep him in touch with the results of research and speculation; and his writings served, for the first time, to popularize scientific knowledge in France.

After composing some indifferent operas, pastorals, and novels he lent his weight to the cause of the Moderns in their struggle with the Ancients by his *Dialogues des Morts* (1683), perhaps the most common-sense contribution to that literary controversy. His argument was that the extolling of the Ancients was generally a device for discrediting one's contemporaries. The Ancients, he thought, had the inestimable advantage that as they came before us they said many things in a manner difficult to improve upon; but this excellence was confined to a narrow sphere, namely, to poetry and eloquence. The Moderns, on the other hand, have this advantage, that they can start where their predecessors left off, and so each generation enters into a heritage which continues steadily to augment:

A man of culture is, as it were, compounded from the distillations of all the cultures of preceding ages. Such a man will have no old age; for men do not degenerate, and there will be a steady accumulation of sanity and wisdom as one age succeeds the other.

This apparently commonplace remark was of startling novelty when first enunciated; for, in common with religion, both learning and literature looked to the past for their models, and thought of decline as identical with retrogression from these models. Fontenelle's doctrine, trite as it may seem to us, was more original than any advanced by the thinkers of either Reformation or Renaissance; for it helped not merely to change human outlook, but to reverse it; since civilization was thought of no longer as a downward path leading away from heights of revelation and inspiration, but as an upward and widening road, quarried out by long successions of pioneers. Moreover, this was an optimistic creed; it implied a faith in humanity and purpose, an attitude of mind destined to exercise a profound influence on the thought of succeeding centuries.

Fontenelle was indifferent to religious and philosophical systems; he thought that, while most men made their gods as foolish as themselves, they were inconsistent enough to deny reason to the brute creation. They were mostly fools, but progressive fools. Only by gazing at the heavens intelligently could they realize the infinite pettiness of their bickerings. Such was the moral of his *Entretiens sur la pluralité des mondes* (1686), the first popular account of astronomy, an indirect but devastating criticism of the doctrine of *Le Roi soleil*. Its readableness familiarized Parisian society with a new contrast—that between the infinite and the infinitesimal—and its date of publication coincided with that of a far more important but less popular work, Newton's *Principia*, which was later to be introduced to the inexpert French reader in the 'vulgarizations' of Voltaire. Thus an entirely new universe was brought within human ken; old miracles were displaced by wonders more startling and more easily authenticated, and at one bound the narrow horizons of human life were completely swept away. It was a revolution all the more ominous because it was silent.

With age, Fontenelle acquired even greater conviction and tranquillity. He came to believe in the immutability of the laws of nature and the essential solidarity of the sciences; also he kept his views above the level of controversy by refusing to reply to Jesuit attacks; so in this way the gulf which separated the old traditions from the new science was in France recognized to be impassable. Among Fontenelle's friends and contemporaries was one whose opinions reveal the same originality, coupled with a reasoned maturity: the abbé de Saint-Pierre. Charles Irenée Castel, abbé de Saint-Pierre (1658–1743), was, like Fénelon, a man of noble family and, like Voltaire and Buffon, a pupil of the Jesuits. His wealth relieved him from the necessity of making a livelihood, and his prolonged old age gave weight and dignity to the salons which he frequented. As faithfully as a barometer he recorded changes in the pressure of the intellectual atmosphere around him; for he left theology for science, science for ethics, and ethics for politics, never once diverging from the sustained seriousness and purposefulness which animated his whole career. Cardinal Fleury, a shrewd judge,

summed him up as '*un politique triste et désastreux*'; a verdict true to this
extent that Saint-Pierre was always concocting schemes for the
benefit of humanity, and the cardinal-statesmen of France were
naturally suspicious of anything which threatened to disturb the
established order of things.

Sometimes a new philosophy can be summed up and popularized
in a word or phrase; it was so with Bentham and Saint-Pierre. The
one brought into vogue the conception of utility, the other gave a
new life to the word *bienfaisance*. Thus in literature Saint-Pierre
thought that the true criterion was not the aesthetic but the useful;
biographies should depict the achievements not merely of the great
but of the good. This he illustrated in his *Annales Politiques* where he
praised Colbert for his reforms and condemned Louis XIV for
his aggressions. Henry IV he thought a great king because he
restored order and peace after the Wars of Religion; wars of
conquest he considered were wars of destruction. True greatness
might be either of the speculative or the practical order; the one
devising schemes for the improvement of the human race, the
other applying them; in this way he advocated an entirely novel
standard of values. He believed in progress through education, and
that education should be one of the first concerns of the State.
He was concerned not with the truth of Christian doctrines, but
with their utility; and in priests he saw not the exponents of dogma,
but possible teachers of ethics. Thus in religion he found not a
means of ensuring salvation in the next life, but a means of securing
social amelioration in this.

Most remarkable perhaps of his many projects was that outlined
in the *Projet de Paix Perpetuelle*, which he commenced in 1713. The
inspiration of this scheme for perpetual peace was derived from the
Memoirs of Sully, the minister of Henry IV, who had attributed to
his master the intention of combining the European powers into a
federation for the purpose of limiting war to that with the Turks
and settling national disputes by arbitration. Sully's *Memoirs*
probably contained nearly as much fancy as fact, but they served
nevertheless to provide a basis on which the later doctrines of
peace and disarmament could be imposed. It was Saint-Pierre who
made these doctrines of practical moment. He had sufficient faith
to believe that war would one day disappear from civilization, and
that as men discarded outworn fetishes, so governments would

abandon the view that nations are to each other as rival packs of wolves. This tradition of perpetual peace, derived from the reputed designs of a great king, was amplified and popularized by the enthusiasm of Saint-Pierre, and was left as a philosophic legacy to Rousseau, Kant, and Bentham. A disillusioned world may give these idealists the lie; but it is a poor age in which there is no hope, and it was on this note of confidence in a greater and happier future that the literature of Louis XIV's reign was brought to its close.

Conclusion

LOUIS XIV DIED on 20 August 1715, leaving the throne to a great-grandson of five years. On its way to the burying-place of French kings at Saint-Denis the funeral cortège was insulted by the mob; but this was no more than a local demonstration; for the nation regarded the great monarch with veneration, and lavished its affection on the child who was afterwards to rule as Louis XV. Throughout the greater part of the eighteenth century the reputation of Louis remained high with noble, philosopher, and *bourgeois*; and in 1752 the French Academy set this subject for a prize poem: *La tendresse de Louis XIV pour sa famille*. With a touch of kindly irony, Montesquieu in his *Lettres Persanes* pictured him as the magician of the west, able to conduct war on funds raised by the sale of titles, and exercising his empire over even the minds of his subjects, '*il les fait penser comme il veut*'; more sincere was the admiration of Voltaire, as agile in forcing his way into royal society as in escaping from it, who acclaimed the age of Louis XIV as '*le plus éclairé qui fut jamais*', and depicted Madame de Montespan in a manner which won the approval of Madame de Pompadour. To the age of enlightenment and benevolent despots the reign of Louis XIV had at least this commendation; that it was one of ceaseless activity, directed by one all-controlling mind, activity which brought the whole civilized world within its scope; its grandeur could therefore be contrasted with the apathy and viciousness which distinguished the Court of Louis XV in his mature years. For long, Frenchmen looked back with pride and regret on *Le Grand Siècle*, so full of stirring events and great men, so symbolic of the domination of French culture and arms.

That this should be so is a striking tribute to the veneration in which the monarchy was held during the greater part of the *Ancien Régime*. The sufferings of France, the mistakes of Louis's policy, the cost and fruitlessness of his wars, the crime of the expulsion of the Huguenots; any one of these would be more than enough to ruin a ministry; but all of them were forgotten in the glamour conjured up by the creator of Versailles; for France, the most logical nation in the world, had been completely hypnotized by Louis XIV. Compared with the profusion and expansiveness of his rule, every other dominion seemed petty and mean; other nations might populate continents or win markets, but France had cowed nations and seized provinces. It was for this reason that the loss of Canada in the Seven Years War seemed to be adequately compensated for by the acquisition of Corsica and Lorraine. But though Louis enhanced rather than diminished the reputation of the French monarchy, he nevertheless undermined it; in the words of a great French historian (Lavisse), 'he used it up'. That only a shell was left came to be gradually realized in the eighteenth century; disillusionment was the inevitable result, all the greater because the passion for monarchy had been so strong. Men began to speak in whispers as if beginning to suspect that they had been deceived; by the end of Louis XV's reign (1774) the whispers had become outspoken comment; and the unfortunate Louis XVI offered the pathetic spectacle of a monarch anxious to satisfy every popular demand. His irresolution was the final disillusionment; his good intentions merely served to set off in sharper contrast the corrupt edifice of which he was the titular head. Only by the complete demolition of that edifice could men hope to build anew.

It is inevitable that in post-Revolutionary France the reputation of Louis should have suffered some diminution; and it is noteworthy that the archivist, Mignet, in his preface to a monumental collection of the diplomatic correspondence of Louis and his agents used the phrase 'a lack of intelligence' of the various policies which the King pursued. Subsequent French historians have commented on this lack of sequence or consistency in the foreign policy of Louis XIV; and the majority of them have frankly confessed their conviction that the reign was a misfortune for France and Europe. They have stigmatized the conduct of those such as Bossuet and Louvois who pandered to the weak or vicious elements in the royal

character; they have condemned the Revocation of the Edict of
Nantes as worse than a blunder; and they have deplored the fact
that, though Louis added Franche Comté to his frontier possessions,
he nevertheless left France more insecure than he found it. Such
writers, while paying tribute to the literary and artistic glories of
Versailles and the spread of French culture among the upper
classes of Europe, set against these things the impoverishment of
France, the pursuit of a selfish and personal policy, and the creation
of hatreds which had to be avenged.

In England, a somewhat more favourable view has generally
been adopted. Louis has been credited with far-sightedness, with
zeal for the interests of his country; his diplomacy has repeatedly
been acclaimed as a most brilliant intellectual achievement, because
it always gained its immediate objects, and served to divide a world
of enemies; his wars have been condoned on the ground that they
were intended to strengthen French frontiers, or because they
enhanced French prestige; his treatment of the Huguenots has been
fathered on the clergy; his invasion of Holland and his devastations
of the Palatinate have been attributed to Louvois. Special emphasis
has been laid on the royal industry, regularity, piety, and devotion
to the duties of kingship, possibly because these qualities are not
often found together in kings. More generally, it has been felt by
some historians that such high rank, such long wars, such great
buildings, and such towering dominance at home and abroad attest
not only the great king, but the great man; and where the moral
conduct of Louis has incurred stricture, there has commonly been
adduced in mitigation these two uncontested facts; his good intentions and his implicit faith in God.

More important than posthumous reputations are the standards
of value by which men gauge the achievements of the past. On
oriental standards Louis must rank high; for he was infinitely
greater as destroyer than as creator; he had no mean between the
extremes of barbaric profusion and rudimentary cunning; he
was something exotic and primitive in his western world. It needed
only the brilliance of his Court and the omnipotence of his rule to
transform Louis the man into Louis the cult. In terms of this cult the
progress of civilization is inseparable from military conquest, and
the ruler becomes the personification of a vindictive and irritable
nationalism to be appeased only by aggression and devastation.

However suitable to conditions in ancient Asia, this ideal acquires sinister possibilities in an age of high explosives and increased economic interdependence, when war, so far from promoting civilization, threatens to end it.

This fact may temper enthusiasm for the cult of the *Grand Monarque*. In proportion as personal caprice and thirst for military glory cease to determine the inter-relations of civilized states, so discredit will be cast on those altars whereon such lavish sacrifice was offered by Louis XIV.

Selected Further Reading

1. Standard Histories of the Reign
E. LAVISSE, *Louis XIV, 1643–85*, vol. VII: 1 and 2 of *Histoire de France depuis les origines jusqu'à la Révolution*, 1905–6.

P. SAGNAC and A. DE SAINT-LÉGER, *Louis XIV, 1661–1715*, vol. X of *Peuples et Civilisations*, 3rd ed., 1949 (the first ed. of 1935 had the title *La Prépondérance française: Louis XIV, 1661–1715*).

E. PRÉCLIN and V.-L. TAPIÉ, *Le XVIIe Siècle*, vol. VII: 1 in the series '*Clio: Introduction aux études historiques*', 2nd rev. ed., 1949.

R. MOUSNIER, *Les XVIe et XVIIe Siècles*, vol. IV of *Histoire générale des civilisations*, 1954 (3rd ed. 1961).

The New Cambridge Modern History, vol. V: *The Ascendancy of France, 1648–1688*, ed. F. L. Carsten, 1961.

2. Biographies of Louis XIV
H. CARRÉ, *L'Enfance et la première jeunesse de Louis XIV*, 1944, transl., *The Early Life of Louis XIV 1638–1661*, 1951.

G. LACOUR-GAYET, *L'Éducation politique de Louis XIV*, 2nd ed., 1923.

H. MÉTHIVIER, *Louis XIV* (No. 426 in '*Que sais-je?*' series), 1950 (3rd ed. 1962).

W. H. LEWIS, *Louis XIV, an informal portrait*, 1959.

P. ERLANGER, *Louis XIV*, 1960.

G. MONGRÉDIEN, *Louis XIV*, 1963.

3. English Histories of France
J. LOUGH, *An Introduction to Seventeenth-Century France*, 1954.

G. R. R. TREASURE, *Seventeenth-Century France*, 1966.

4. Diplomacy and Foreign Policy
G. C. PICAVET, *La Diplomatie française au temps de Louis XIV, 1661–1715*, 1930.

L. ANDRÉ, *Louis XIV et l'Europe*, 1950.

G. ZELLER, *De Louis XIV à 1789*, vol. III: 2 in *Histoire des relations internationales*, 1955. This should be supplemented by the double issue, Nos. 46–47, of the periodical *XVIIe Siècle*, 1960, devoted to *Problèmes de politique étrangère sous Louis XIV*.

5. Social and economic life

P. BOISSONNADE, *Colbert, le Triomphe de l'Étatisme, 1661–83*, 1932.

C. W. COLE, *Colbert and a Century of French Mercantilism*, 2 vols., 1939; and the same author's *French Mercantilism, 1683–1700*, 1943.

XVIIe Siècle, Nos. 70–71 (double issue), 1966, devoted to *Aspects de l'économie française au XVIIe siècle.*

J. SAINT-GERMAIN, *Les Financiers sous Louis XIV*, 1950.

W. C. SCOVILLE, *The Persecution of the Huguenots and French Economic Development, 1680–1720*, 1960.

H. LÜTHY, *La Banque Protestante de la Révocation de l'Édit de Nantes à la Révolution*, Vol. I: *1685–1730*, 1961.

P. SAGNAC, *La société et la monarchie absolue (1661–1715)*, vol. I of *La Formation de la société française moderne*, 1945.

P. GOUBERT, *Beauvais et le Beauvaisis de 1600 à 1730. Contribution à l'histoire de la France du XVIIe siècle*, 1960 (2 parts); or the same author's *Louis XIV et vingt millions de français*, 1966.

G. MONGRÉDIEN, *La vie quotidienne au temps de Louis XIV*, 1948.

6. Literature, Art, Science, Ideas

A. ADAM, *Histoire de la littérature française au XVIIe Siècle*, 5 vols., 1948–62.

W. D. HOWARTH, *Life and Letters in France*, vol. I: *The Seventeenth Century*, 1965.

P. HAZARD, *La crise de la conscience européenne, 1680–1715*, 1935, transl., *The European Mind*, 1953.

P. DE NOLHAC, *Versailles et la cour de France: l'Art de Versailles*, 1930.

SIR ANTHONY BLUNT, *Art and Architecture in France, 1500–1700*, 1953.

L. HAUTECOEUR, *Louis XIV, Roi Soleil*, 1953.

V.-L. TAPIÉ, *Baroque et classicisme*, 1957; transl., *The Age of Grandeur*, 1960.

R.-A. WEIGERT, *L'Epoque Louis XIV*, 1962.

H. BROWN, *Scientific Organisations in Seventeenth-Century France, 1620–80*, 1934.

P. MOUY, *Le développement de la physique cartésienne, 1646–1712*, 1934.

H. KIRKINEN, *Les origines de la conception moderne de l'homme-machine: le problème de l'âme en France à la fin du règne de Louis XIV (1670–1715)*, 1960.

7. Religious Questions

N. ABERCROMBIE, *The Origins of Jansenism*, 1936.

G. H. DODGE, *The Political Theory of the Huguenots of the Dispersion*, 1947.

G. GUITTON, *Le Père de la Chaize, confesseur de Louis XIV*, 2 vols., 1959.

J. ORCIBAL, *Louis XIV contre Innocent XI*, 1949; and the same author's *Louis XIV et les Protestants*, 1951.

A.-G. MARTIMORT, *Le Gallicanisme de Bossuet*, 1953.

J. COGNET, *Le Jansénisme* (No. 960 in 'Que sais-je?' series), 1961.

XVIIe Siècle, No. 25, 1955, devoted to religious issues.

8. French Institutions and Administrations

Études sur l'histoire administrative et sociale de l'ancien régime, ed. G. Pagès,

1938; supplemented by two double issues of *XVIIe Siècle*: Nos. 42–43, 1959, devoted to *Serviteurs du roi*, and Nos. 58–59, 1962, devoted to *Le Droit*.

F. L. FORD, *Robe and Sword. The Regrouping of the French Aristocracy after Louis XIV*, 1953.

G. LIVET, *L'Intendance d'Alsace sous Louis XIV, 1648–1715*, 2 vols., 1953, or 1 vol., 1956.

J. SAINT-GERMAIN, *La Reynie et la police au grand siècle*, 1962.

9. Military and Naval History

L. ANDRÉ, *Michel Le Tellier et l'organisation de l'armée monarchique*, 1906; and the same author's *Michel Le Tellier et Louvois*, 1942.

G. ZELLER, *L'Organisation défensive des frontières du nord et de l'est au XVIIe siècle*, 1928.

G. A. M. GIRARD, *Le Service militaire en France à la fin du règne de Louis XIV, Racolage et Milice (1701–1715)*, 1922.

C. DE LA RONCIÈRE, *Histoire de la marine française*, vols. V and VI, 1930–32.

R. MÉMAIN, *La Marine du Guerre sous Louis XIV: le Matériel*, 1937.

P. BAMFORD, *Forests and French Sea-Power, 1660–1789*, 1956.

E. ASHER, *The Resistance to the Maritime Classes*, 1960.

J. S. BROMLEY, 'The French Privateering War, 1700–1713' in *Historical Essays 1600–1750 presented to David Ogg* (edd. H. E. Bell and R. L. Ollard), 1963, pp. 203–31.

A. DE WISMES, *Jean Bart et la Guerre de Course*, 1964.

10. France Overseas

S. MIMS, *Colbert's West Indian Policy*, 1912.

M. GIRARD, *Histoire de la Louisiane française*, I: *Le Règne de Louis XIV 1698–1715*, 1953.

M. TRUDEL, *Atlas Historique du Canada français*, 1961.

W. J. ECCLES, *Canada under Louis XIV, 1663–1701*, 1964.

11. Bibliographies and Historiographical Studies

E. BOURGEOIS and L. ANDRÉ, *Les Sources de l'histoire de France*, vols. III and IV: *Louis XIV*, 1926–35.

S. HONORÉ, *Catalogue général des livres imprimés de la Bibliothèque Nationale. Actes Royaux*, vols. III and IV: *Louis XIV*, 1946–50.

P. DE VRIES, *Het Beeld van Lodewijk XIV in de Franse Geschiedschrijving* (with a French summary), 1948.

W. F. CHURCH, *The Greatness of Louis XIV—Myth or Reality?*, 1959.

J. B. WOLF, 'The reign of Louis XIV: a selected bibliography of writings since the war of 1914–18', *Journal of Modern History*, XXXVI (1964).

H. G. JUDGE, *Louis XIV*, 1965, pp. 121–130.

R. M. HATTON

Index